TRUE OR FALSE?

- A 3-ounce vodka martini contains 188 calories and no nutritional value.
- Traces of pesticide are not unusual in table wines.
- Chemical additives are common in whiskey, rum, gin, vodka, scotch, and most commercially produced hard liquors.
- A possible link has been established between sperm damage and heavy drinking in men.
- Pregnant women who drink can endanger the lives of their unborn children.

The answer to all these is *TRUE*.

If you don't know what happens to alcohol as it passes through your system—and, more important, what happens to your system—your health could depend on the vital facts revealed in ALCOHOL AND NUTRITION.

OTHER PYRAMID PUBLICATIONS
BY GARY NULL

BIOFEEDBACK, FASTING & MEDITATION

FOOD COMBINING HANDBOOK

HANDBOOK OF SKIN AND HAIR

PROTEIN FOR VEGETARIANS

SUCCESSFUL PREGNANCY

ALCOHOL and NUTRITION

GARY & STEVE NULL

PYRAMID PUBLICATIONS NEW YORK

ALCOHOL AND NUTRITION

A PYRAMID BOOK

Pyramid edition published February 1977

Library of Congress Catalog Card Number: 76-43188

Printed in the United States of America

Pyramid Books are published by Pyramid Publications (Harcourt Brace Jovanovich, Inc.). Its trademarks, consisting of the word "Pyramid" and the portrayal of a pyramid, are registered in the United States Patent Office.

PYRAMID PUBLICATIONS
(Harcourt Brace Jovanovich, Inc.)
757 Third Avenue, New York, N.Y. 10017

Table of Contents

ALCOHOL and NUTRITION

INTRODUCTION

The intent of this book is to present a well-rounded, objective picture of the effects of alcohol on the body, how it can cause disease, how it affects our social environment, and why we drink it.

There are many reasons for using alcohol, and the vast majority of users are not in any danger from it. Nevertheless, alcoholism and alcohol abuse is extremely prevalent in our society. This use is not unique to our culture, of course. Drinking alcoholic beverages to alter states of consciousness is almost as ancient as man himself. It has been used for this purpose in many cultures and societies. But, as with most pleasures, overindulgence in alcohol can be harmful.

We are living in a stress-filled society. And there are as many ways of combating stress as there are people. While much attention has been focused upon the widespread use of such drugs as marijuana, amphetamines and LSD, very little attention has been paid to the most consistently abused drug of all—alcohol. And this drug *is* abused, in spite of the fact that it is relatively respectable and generally "legal." Nearly half of all traffic deaths and a third of all murder victims show significant amounts of alcohol in their bloodstreams. It is also a fact that heavy users of alcohol may shorten their life spans by as much as ten to twelve years. Roughly nine million people in the United States have alcohol-related problems, and approximately $25 billion a year is spent combating the effects of alcohol misuse.

Most Americans drink. We are a drinking society, and there is no use denying it. It is the American norm. It is learned at home and from friends. But there doesn't seem to be any particularly American drinking pattern or attitude toward alcoholic consumption.

How much we drink, how often, are things which vary greatly with age, sex, religion, ethnic origins, education, occupation, and emotional stability. Some people have a drink every day. Indeed, some get drunk every day. Many individuals live close to a drinking problem. Almost one-in-five persons report that someone close to them drinks too much.

It is thought that upper class, educated urbanites are the most consistent drinkers, but in truth the poor and the young have the greatest drinking problems. Heavy drinking and its difficulties seem to center around the ages of eighteen to twenty-five—the unsettled years, the years of leaving the security of the family and before a new family has been established. This seems to change as an individual grows older, however, and in many cases often results in abstinence. Unfortunately, it can also result in alcoholism.

A bibliography and a list of additional reading material is provided at the end of each chapter and at the end of the book. In some cases, studies are credited in the text rather than in the bibliography. This material was of great help in preparing this book.

Alcohol in moderate amounts can be a wonderful tranquilizer. But it can also create incredible havoc in the human system. As you read, you will see how.

James Dawson

CHAPTER ONE

ALCOHOL: What It Is And Why We Drink It

Man stumbled onto alcohol in pre-history, probably very early in his development. Archaelogical records of even the earliest civilizations show the presence of various beverages that could induce euphoria, intoxication, sedation and narcosis.

Relatively primitive agricultural peoples were able to make beer. Their method was simple. Tribal brewers chewed grain and spit into a prepared mash. An enzyme from their mouths converted the starch from the grain into sugar, which in turn fermented and produced alcohol. From this, it was only a short step to the discovery that fruits and grains were not the only natural substances that could be converted into alcohol. Flowers and cactuses were variously used, as well as milk, honey and the saps of trees.

There is considerable evidence that early man assigned magical properties to alcoholic beverages. In some cultures this magical liquid was controlled exclusively by certain priests, dispensed as a reward for bravery in battle, or perhaps to instill bravery before battle. No doubt our primitive, superstitious ancestors felt that the altered perception of an alcoholic glow was some sort of religious experience.

By the time history reached the written tablet, entire civilizations were using alcohol in large quantities, and alcoholism had become a problem. The ancient Greeks and Hebrews, the Medes and Persians, the Indians and the Chinese, bemoaned alcoholism as a plague. The problem was of such concern to some societies that early attempts at prohibition were not uncommon, but they were generally as unsuccessful as our own "noble experiment" of the 1920's.

ALCOHOL DISTILLATION

Ethyl alcohol, or *ethanol,* is the principal ingredient in all alcoholic beverages. It is the only member of the alcohol family that can be ingested by human beings. Other alcohols, such as *methyl alcohol* and *isopropyl,* or rubbing alcohol, are toxic. They can cause internal damage or death. In this discussion ethanol is what we refer to as "alcohol".

Until the fifteenth century, wines and beers contained no more than 14 per cent alcohol because a higher percentage would kill the yeasts that produce natural fermentation. But as more sophisticated distillation techniques were developed, stronger beverages could be produced.

Experiments with distillation techniques in the fifteenth century first produced the "spirit" of wine we now call brandy. As the floodgates opened, the "spirits" of other alcohol beverages were discovered in quick succession. Distillers learned how to produce liquors that were 50 per cent alcohol rather than the 6 to 14 per cent which was common earlier. Naturally these beverages were in great demand. Everything that could be achieved by drinking weaker beverages could also be achieved to a much greater degree by drinking spirits.

For a while, alcohol was hailed as the great savior of mankind, earning a place in medieval pharmacopeia as the mythical *aqua vitae,* or "water of life." Alcohol was thought to cure almost any disease or affliction. Needless to say, all it could do was obliterate pain and physical discomfort, but this property was enough to sustain its popularity.

ALCOHOL AS FOOD

Alcohol is an efficient food. Indeed, in some primitive societies it served as a valuable adjunct to the diet. This happened mainly because primitive brewing techniques, those used before the invention of distillation, preserved the vitamin and mineral content of the fermenting food substances. This is not true of "brewed" beverages today, or of any liquid that has undergone distillation. Modern brewing technology completely destroys every dietary property in alcohol except one—calories.

Alcohol is fattening. Any weight-conscious adult knows this. But this does not mean that alcohol is nutritious. The calories in most alcoholic beverages are known as "empty" calories. They provide no nutritional benefits. An 8-ounce glass of beer contains 112 calories and 10.6 grams of carbohydrate; a 3-ounce vodka martini contains 188 calories and no carbohydrates; the same size daiquiri has 190 calories, 9.5 grams of carbohydrate.[21] Scotch, bourbon, and gin have approximately 105 calories per 1½ oz. shot.[22] None of these calories contains any nutritional elements to sustain health!

Additives. Like any modern foods, alcoholic beverages are loaded with additives. In most cases these are not harmful, but occasionally they can be deadly. Take, for instance, the case of the cobalt deaths in the mid-sixties. Heavy beer drinkers in the United States and Canada suddenly began to die of severe heart damage for no apparent reason. The only characteristic that these people seemed to share was a taste for large quantities of beer. Investigators immediately went to work on beer contaminants and ferreted out a culprit—cobalt.

Cobalt is not a natural component of beer. It is a metal that *is* necessary to the human body in minute quantities. However, like arsenic, cobalt in larger amounts can be deadly. It had been added to create a big "head" to make the beer more visually attractive in the glass after it had been poured. Forty-seven people died.[14] Cobalt was finally outlawed by the FDA after it was directly connected to these deaths.

In 1971 another additive commonly used in beer was found to be dangerous. The substance, *diethylpyrocarbonate, or DEPC*, was developed in Germany in the mid-fifties. It was intended as a preservative agent. DEPC was considered to be completely safe as it breaks down into water and carbon dioxide, two substances that are themselves components of life. In 1971, however, two Swedish scientists discovered that DEPC molecules react with the trace amounts of ammonia, which are found in all beverages, to form a chemical called *urethane*. Urethane is a well-known carcinogen, or cancer-causing agent. When investigators began to probe into the use of this chemical, they found that almost everyone in the industry denied using it. DEPC was banned by the FDA in 1972.[14] But there are still many chemical additives used in beer.

The reader may already be aware of the scandal generated by the revelation of the dubious practices of certain French wine producers. It was discovered that respected members of the French wine industry had been doctoring their wines: improving the color, mixing different types of wines in order to improve taste, and chemically tampering with a product traditionally thought to be pure.

It is well known that vintners have been using additives in their wines for many years, yet their advertising has continually emphasized the purity of wine and maintained the myth of the "old family vintners" who have been using the same winemaking techniques for generations. The fact is that there are over seventy chemical additives that are permitted to be added to wine, some of which go into the wine during the brewing process itself. Others are added after fermentation has taken place, prior to bottling.

Asbestos is a popular wine-filtering agent. It is also a dangerous air pollutant and has recently been linked to cancer by a widely publicized water pollution case in the Great Lakes region. Asbestos fibers are not expelled from the body by natural processes. They remain in the system, and scar tissue forms around them. Proof of the dangers of asbestos can be seen in the case of individuals who work in asbestos-producing plants. Many of these people get asbestos into their lungs and develop *mesothelomia*, a cancer of the lung. Asbestos in minute quantities is frequently found in popular wines, an unsettling fact when one considers that asbestos is thought to be a cause of cancer of the digestive system.

A brief mention should also be made of pesticides. They regularly find their way into wine as a result of sprays used on wine grapes as they are growing.

WHY DO WE DRINK ALCOHOL?

Little is known about why certain individuals become dependant on alcohol. A few of the current theories are presented below.

Relatively few studies on alcohol appetite have been conducted. One of the earliest of these took place at the University of Chile, in Santiago in 1941. In this study, rats were offered a free choice between water and alcohol and the daily intake of each was carefully measured. In some instances specific alcohol concentrations were used. These allowed the researchers to compare alcohol ingestion to body weight. In other instances different concentrations were made available in order to determine whether or not the rats would develop a taste for any particular strength. The results were startling. It was found that the rats preferred alcohol over water, particularly those animals who exhibited a deficiency of B-complex vitamins. This led directly to the hypothesis that alcoholism might be related to nutritional deficiencies in the diet.[5] Some researchers have subsequently claimed alcoholic cures by changing their patients' eating habits. Later animal studies have upheld these claims by reporting that rats reduce their alcoholic intake when provided with vitamins and *glutamine*, the product of a nonessential acid and ammonia.[17]

When the body exhibits a thiamin (a B-complex vitamin) deficiency, an increase in alcohol consumption frequently occurs, along with a drop in food intake. Why this comes about is not clear. What it does, however, is lower the number of useful calories available to the body. Since the calories in alcohol can replace many of these useful calories, the problem is compounded.

Whether or not these findings have any connection with the problems of alcoholism in man is not clear. Obviously, few, if any, human alcoholics drink because the beverage simply tastes good. Indeed, most of us are familiar with the type of alcoholic that will drink *any* alcoholic beverage, even poisonous ones such as rubbing alcohol or canned heat.

Jorge Mardones, of the University of Chile, has suggested that the desire for alcohol might in some way be linked with the desire for energy.[5] Experiments designed to establish this theory have shown that alcohol is sought as an energy source only when other forms of energy-giving foods are not available.

R. J. Williams proposed an allergy theory in 1959. He suggested that the answer might lie in the natural function of the hypothalamus gland, which regulates the body's needs. He also suggested that there might be

18

a complex that controls the body's consumption of alcohol, just as there is a complex that controls consumption of food and water. If this control center were to be disturbed in any way, by the excessive consumption of alcohol, for instance, an insatiable appetite for alcohol could result.[6] So far, there has been no experimental support for this theory.

Another hypothesis is that alcoholism might result from an endocrine disorder, perhaps a pituitary deficiency. Using this as a basis, some researchers have suggested a treatment for alcoholism based on hormone supplements. Unfortunately, little scientific evidence has been offered in support of this contention.

ALCOHOL AND ENVIRONMENTAL PRESSURES

Although there is increasing speculation that alcoholism is a physically based disease, there can be no doubt that the environmental pressures surrounding all of us contribute to the problem. There is often a desire, even among individuals who have no particular liking for the taste of alcohol, to escape from such outside stresses as high achievement goals, job pressures and city living. Alcohol provides us with the means for this escape. What is unfortunate is that many who take advantage of the tranquilizing effects of alcohol are those who are least able to handle the consequences.

Alcohol consumption in the United States has reached an extremely high level. Between 1960 and 1970 per capita consumption of alcohol rose over 25 per cent. It now exceeds the point reached during the days of prohibition. One in ten of the ninety million or so Americans who drink are considered problem drinkers. In addition, a large number of this group are under the age of twenty-one.[9]

What has caused this increase? Why can one individual comfortably drink a martini or an aperitif before dinner and show no ill effects, while another individual seems to undergo a total personality change? The answers to these questions still elude us. All that is definitely known is that for those people most susceptible to overconsumption of alcohol, the social pressures behind excessive drinking are immense.

In many homes hospitality is characterized by offering a drink. Some hosts hardly take a guest's coat before placing a drink in the hand. Also, in some social strata, it is believed that heavy drinking is considered a sign of masculinity. This can be especially disturbing to the young male who is struggling to establish his sexual identity. It can provide a powerful stimulus toward establishing drinking habits that can prove harmful in later life.

And, of course, we are living in a period when many traditional values and customs are vanishing. Many individuals are unable to cope with this and turn to alcohol for escape. An example of this might be the American Indian. As more and more tribal lands were usurped, and as the traditional roles of hunter and warrior became less and less significant with no useful opportunities for change, many Indians turned to alcohol for forgetfulness.

Nor is this problem unique to the United States. France, for example, where it is acceptable for even children to drink wine on a daily basis, is believed to have the highest degree of alcoholism in the world. Fully 10 per cent of the population is conservatively rated as alcoholic. Russia also has a nationwide alcohol problem. Soviet newspapers blame fully 60 per cent of the nation's accidents and fatalities on alcoholism.[9]

A surprising contrast is found in the case of orientals and alcohol. For years, western observers have been baffled by the incredibly low rate of alcoholism in oriental societies. It was first thought that this could be explained by a different set of cultural values. The Chinese, for instance, frown on public displays of drunkenness.

There is new evidence, however, that this difference might be genetic.

Dr. John Ewing, working at the University of North Carolina, has recently announced some fascinating new findings. Dr. Ewing selected a group of forty-eight subjects, half of whom were of oriental origin and half of European stock. These volunteers were first given a cocktail of ethyl alcohol and ginger ale, the amount being determined by each subject's body weight. After this drink, the subjects were interviewed for two hours in order to gauge the effects of the alcohol. The subjects of European descent became relaxed, comfortable and happy, while the oriental group became anxious and dizzy. These last symptoms were also accompanied by a pounding in the head, muscular weakness, and a tendency to blush severely almost immediately after drinking. Seventeen of the twenty-four reacted in this manner, while only three in the other group showed this result. The heartbeat and blood pressure of the orientals also showed a marked change almost immediately—their heart rate increased more rapidly and their blood pressure dropped more sharply.

An interesting note is that the blood level of a chemical known as *acetaldehyde* rose in the oriental subjects. This chemical is an antiseptic and an anesthetic, and Dr. Ewing feels that it may be the key to the uncomfortable reaction experienced by orientals when they drink.

This report suggested in conclusion that since alcohol made orientals uncomfortable, creating tension and causing anxiety, it was not likely that they would develop alcoholism. The westerners felt more comfortable with alcohol. It made them feel good. This could lead to excessive drinking.[1]

The problem also seems to exist among other ethnic groups. Some statistics seem to indicate that Blacks and Chicanos are particularly prone to heavy drinking. This may be at least partly explained by the problems associated with differing life styles and the stress of poverty that these minority groups must often combat.[19]

Some Irishmen are also known for being heavy drinkers and are quick to brag about it. The reason is not clear, although some researchers feel that a major contributing factor is that Irish-American social life so often centers around the neighborhood pub.[18]

The lowest incidence of alcoholism among Americans of ethnic extraction is found among the Jews. This can be partly explained by the Jewish proscription against public drunkenness, and a life style that is more oriented toward food than drink.[20]

Obviously, the causes of alcoholism are complex. Social customs almost certainly contribute to this problem as they reinforce and encourage those who show a natural inclination to drink. But why do many people exhibit such tendencies? More and more there is additional evidence that the answer might lie in genetics. The oriental reaction to alcohol is supportive of this contention.

There is as yet no direct evidence that genetic deficiencies are responsible for alcoholism. Many researchers are beginning to admit, however, that there could be some as yet undetermined physical factor that might make one human more susceptible to alcoholism than another.

Drinking patterns. Drinking patterns vary widely; from the total abstinence of the Moslem to the almost universal acceptance of alcohol by the French, alcohol intake almost defies classification. In many societies, individuals drink primarily at home, while in others, the home may be the only place a person doesn't drink. In some countries drinking is almost religious ritual, while in others it is restricted to formal situations.

Conditions that contribute to these patterns also vary greatly. An individual's taste, psychological need, sex, age, geographical area, education, associations, religious beliefs, socioeconomic status all contribute in different ways to patterns of drinking. In the United States almost one-third of the adult population are total abstainers. There is also some evidence supporting a connection between educational level and drinking. The higher the level, the more likely it is that an individual will drink. On the other hand it appears that drinking among the more disadvantaged is more likely to be excessive.

In the United States, where drinking problems and trends are more carefully studied and documented than in other countries, there are few recognizable patterns. Americans seem to possess no typical attitude toward alcohol. This may be because Americans have such a wide variety of cultural backgrounds.

In spite of this, there *are* some generalizations that can be made. For instance, the number of abstainers has decreased. Also, recent studies show that 77 per cent of the males in the United States drink compared with 60 per cent of the females. Fifty-seven per cent and 43 per cent of male and female adolescents also drink. These percentages increase as the average age of the subject increases until, during the years between ages twenty-one and twenty-nine, a peak is reached This seems to indicate that during the unsettled years, those years when many of us are searching out the meanings and directions of our lives, a certain amount of alcoholic release is desirable as well as pleasurable. This peak declines as individuals begin their families and settle into a permanent mode of living. It is usually after ths initial period of heavy drinking that many individuals become abstainers.[9]

Rural areas apparently produce more abstainers than urban areas, and more beer drinkers than boozers. This might be attributed to several factors—fewer years of formal education, fundamentalist religious beliefs and more definite religious participation. The exception to this rule, however, is the coal belt that runs through Appalachia, where an urban colonialism

23

created a miserable oppression upon backward, whiskey-making fugitives from Great Britain's slums.

The cocktail party. The cocktail party is a uniquely American institution. Why this is so is not exactly clear, although it has been suggested that it is an outgrowth of the habit of taking a cocktail at the end of a business day. The cocktail party seems to serve as a separator; a way to divide the day into working hours and pleasure hours. Whatever the reason, one thing is certain—the cocktail party may be the most highly organized method of drug abuse in the world.[11]

Boozing at cocktail parties follows a pattern. A drinker has been through a long day. He may be tired, run down, depleted of energy. He consumes one or two drinks in order to loosen up and shrug off stress and anxiety. His tongue gets slippery and the talk begins to flow freely. His body warms up. His face gets slightly numb as the level of alcohol in the blood begins to approach the 10 per cent legal limit for determining intoxication, and the party is reaching its height. Then, drinking slows and the guests begin to leave. Blood alcohol levels drop and conversation begins to pall. The subject's state of consciousness has been altered and the type and degree of that alteration depends upon many things: the rate at which drinks have been consumed; how much is taken; age; body weight; previous drinking experience; whether or not drinking takes place on an empty stomach. If there is no food in the stomach, the alcohol will enter the blood almost immediately.

One cocktail party myth is that a fast drinker gets drunker than a slow drinker. Recently, Ben Morgan Jones and Oscar A. Parsons conducted a study wherein forty male medical students were given a mixture of orange juice and grain alcohol and instructed to finish drinking within fifteen minutes. Some students gulped the mixture down quickly, some sipped it. Though the gulpers absorbed the alcohol faster and acted more intoxicated, blood-level tests proved that all of the students reached the same blood alcohol level at almost the same time, roughly eighty minutes after the test was begun. After this eighty-minute peak, blood alcohol level dropped. The gulpers showed a slower drop than the sippers and they also seemed to be more intoxicated. When Jones and Parsons again performed blood alcohol level tests, nothing had changed. All of the subjects still shared almost identical concentrations of alcohol, even though the sippers seemed more sober than the gulpers. So be warned. Coming home after the cocktail party can be hazardous if you're driving. Even if you are a sipper, you may be legally drunk.[11]

Other Social Factors

Americans drink in groups. They tend to be joiners, connecting themselves with social and professional societies all of which exhibit different drinking patterns. Even individuals of widely varying origins tend to drink in the same manner when in a group. Examples of such groups might be college fraternities or sororities, servicemen, business conventioneers, or guests at a particular type of social function. This is not meant to suggest that individual drinking patterns will not appear. Such patterns always modify social drinking. Even in cases where drinking is completely accepted, such as among the various skid row groups, different patterns are clearly discernable.[8]

An intriguing note is that even among people who drink, which includes the majority of the adult population, many feel that drinking is wrong, either physically or morally. This partly accounts for the many regulations against drinking which drinkers themselves help to legislate.

REFERENCES AND ADDITIONAL READING LIST FOR CHAPTER ONE

1. "Orientals and Alcohol," *Time Magazine*, October 22, 1973.
2. Burgess, Louise Bailey, "Alcohol and Your Health," *Medicine, Science, and Alcohol*, Charles Publishing, Los Angeles, 1973.
3. Milt, Harry, *Basic Handbook on Alcoholism*, Scientific Aids Publication, New Jersey, 1974.
4. Rodgers, D. A., "The Determinants of Alcohol Preference in Animals," *Physiology and Behavior*, Volume 2, Lafayette, Indiana, 1972.
5. Mardones, J., Segovia-Riquelme, N., Varela, A., "Appetite for Alcohol," *Biological Basis for Alcoholism*, Santiago, Chile.
6. Williams, R. J., Berry, L. J., Beerstecher, E., *Individual Alcoholic Patterns, Alcoholism, Genotrophic Diseases*, Proceedings of the National Academy of Sciences, U.S., Vol. 35, No. 6, 1949.
7. Kater, R. M. H., "Differences in the Rate of Ethanol Metabolism in Recently Drinking Alcoholic and Non-drinking Subjects," *The Arkansas Journal of Clinical Nutrition*, Vol. 22, No. 12, December, 1969.
8. Marshall, Pearson, "The Social Environment," *Dynamics of Health and Disease*, 1972.
9. *Alcohol and Health*, U.S. Department of Health, Education and Welfare, Rockville, Maryland, 1971.
10. "Alcoholism: New Victims, New Treatment," *Time Magazine*, April 22, 1974.
11. Jones, Ben Morgan; Parsons, O. A., "Getting High, Coming Down," *Psychology Today*, January, 1975.
12. Jacobsen, E., "The Metabolism of Ethyl Alcohol," *Pharmacological Review*, 4: 107, 1952.
13. Lundquist, F., "Ethanol Alcohol in Blood and Tissue. IV Enzymic Methods." *Methods of Biochemical Analysis*, 7: 240, 1959.

14. Jacobson, M. F., Anderson, J., *Chemical Additives in Booze,* Center for Science in the Public Interest, Washington, D.C., 1972.
15. Muehlberger, C. W., "The Physiological Action of Alcohol," *Journal of the American Medical Association,* 167, 1942.
16. Beerstecher, E., Jr., Reed, I. G., Brown, W. D., Beery, L. J., *The Effect of Single Vitamin Deficiencies on the Consumption of Alcohol by White Rats,* Texas University Publishing, 5109, 115, 1951.
17. Brown, R. V., "Vitamin Deficiency and Voluntary Alcohol Consumption in Mice," *Quarterly Journal of Studies in Alcohol,* 28, 555, 1967.
18. Blane, H. T., "Preliminary Descriptive Data Tabulations of Irish-American and Italian American Drinking Practices Project," Unpublished Paper, January, 1974.
19. Lipscomb, W. R., "Drug Use in a Black Ghetto," *American Journal of Psychology,* 127(9): 1166-1169, 1971.
20. Keller, M., "The Great Jewish Drink Mystery," *British Journal of Addiction,* 1970.
21. Bowes, Anna DePlanter, Church, Charles F., M.D., *Food Values of Portions Commonly Used,* Anna DePlanter Bowes, Philadelphia, Pennsylvania, 1937, 1956.
22. Kaufman, William I., *Brand Name Guide to Calories and Carbohydrates,* Pyramid Books, New York, 1973.

CHAPTER TWO

TWO SIDES OF THE COIN:
Nutrition and Malnutrition

Since we are concerned with nutrition in this book, and since most alcohol-related illnesses and diseases concern malnutrition, it might be a good idea to discuss good nutrition and a healthy body so that we can learn something of how the system utilizes its food when it is functioning properly.

We begin as an egg cell. Once this cell is fertilized it begins to divide, over and over again until we become a collection of the many millions of specialized bits of matter that taken together make us what we are. These cells develop into an organism with almost unlimited potential. But this does not happen immediately, nor does it happen without help—food is needed.

When food elements are supplied to the cells in adequate quantities, the cells mature, and unless there is an accident or a major illness, the organism lives for many years.

There are four requirements for a cell to multiply and remain healthy; oxygen, water, a sympathetic environment, and food. Without these the organism cannot build itself. The first three of these items are easily understood. Understanding how food is used in our bodies is more complicated but vital if we are to remain healthy.

Nutritional needs vary from individual to individual. For example, the nutritional requirements of children are considerably different than adults. More of certain nutriments are needed during childhood than during adulthood.

There are five nutritional elements necessary for cell development and reparation—vitamins; minerals; carbohydrates and sugars, which supply fuel; and protein, which supplies amino acids. Without these the body cannot function. And all of these substances come from outside the body.

MINERALS

There are a number of minerals needed to maintain health. Some are used in minute quantities but are poisonous in large amounts. These include sodium, chlorine, potassium, phosphorous, calcium, iodine, iron, copper, magnesium, manganese, zinc, cobalt, molybdenum, flourine, and some others—*all* of which are required.

VITAMINS

Vitamins are also needed in small amounts as *catalysts,* chemicals used to speed up or initiate a chemical reaction. It would be convenient if only one type of vitamin/catalyst was required, but this is not the case. Many are needed for a variety of different reactions. Without them our bodies would slow down and eventually stop altogether.

Vitamin A (Retinol). This is an oil-soluable vitamin that is toxic in large quantities. It is found in fish-liver oils, egg yoke, butter, cream, fortified margarine, and green leafy or yellow vegetables.

Vitamin D. This is vital for the bone-formation process. It increases calcium and phosphorous absorption. It is found in fish-liver oils, butter, egg yoke, and liver and is produced by the body whenever the skin is stimulated by ultraviolet light.

Vitamin E. This is the so-called miracle vitamin touted as a preventive for everything from impotence to old age. It is found in vegetable oils, wheat germ, leafy vegetables, egg yoke, margarine and legumes.

Vitamin K. The minimum daily requirement of this vitamin has not been established. It is essential, however, in the stimulation of the blood-clotting protein *prothrombin*. It is found in leafy vegetables, pork liver, vegetable oils, and in intestinal flora after the first four days of life.

Vitamin B_1 (thiamin). Thiamin is vital to so many processes that it is difficult to list them. Carbohydrate metabolism is dependent on thiamin, as are central-nerve-cell and heart functions. It is a water-soluble vitamin found in brewer's yeast, whole grains, meat, enriched cereal products, nuts, legumes and potatoes.

Vitamin B_2 (riboflavin). This vitamin is also deeply involved in many bodily processes; carbohydrate metabolsm, energy conversion and the integrity of the mucous membranes. It is found in milk, cheese, meat, liver, eggs, and enriched cereals.

Niacin (nicotinic acid). This is another water-soluble vitamin closely concerned with oxidation. It is also involved in carbohydrate metabolism. Niacin is available from brewer's yeast, liver, meat, fish, legumes, and whole-grain enriched cereal products.

Vitamin B_6 (pyridoxine, pyridoxal and pyridoxamine). This group of vitamins is essential to cellular function and amino and fatty-acid metabolism. It is water-soluble and found in brewer's yeast, organ meats, fish, and whole-grain cereals.

Pantothenic acid (calcium pantothenate). This water-soluble vitamin is involved in fat, protein and carbohydrate metabolism. Its deficiency can cause fatigue, malaise, headache, sleep disturbances, abdominal and muscle cramps, nausea, vomiting and impaired co-ordination. Pantothenic acid is found in brewer's yeast, organ meats, eggs, and legumes.

Folic acid. Folic acid is needed in the proper synthesis of several vital substances. It is found in fresh green leafy vegetables, fruits, organ meats, and brewer's yeast.

Vitamin B_{12}. Vitamin B_{12} is concerned primarily with nerve function and DNA synthesis. It is water-soluble and it is the only vitamin *not* found in any form in vegetables. Its sources are liver, meats, eggs, milk and milk products.

Vitamin C. This may be the most familiar vitamin to most people. It has been widely touted as an aid to prevention of colds. It is vital to the body, particularly in the healing of wounds and the formation of collagen, the protein fiber that makes up practically all body tissue. Vitamin C is water-soluble and is found in citrus fruits, tomatoes, potatoes, cabbage and green peppers.

FUEL

The fuel requirement of our bodies is not very exacting. Fats, sugars and carbohydrates can all be used. Protein can also be used, but it is a last choice. But reliance on the use of alcohol as a fuel is hazardous.

AMINO ACIDS

Amino acids come from proteins. There are many that are vital to the proper functioning of our bodies. These include valine, leucine, isoleucine, methionine, phenylalanine, lycine, theronine, and tryptophan. It is doubtful that one person in fifty has ever heard of these, but they provide the material used in tissue synthesis.

We are now acquainted with some of the more important vitamins, minerals and food elements. It should be emphasized that not only do we need all of these substances, but we need them in proper quantities. In some cases, the proper quantities may be very small. However, less than that specific amount is not only useless, it can also be quite harmful. For example, iodine is a necessary trace element. Only one-thousandth of an ounce of iodine is needed during an entire lifetime. Half of that tiny amount, however, would result in iodine deficiency and thyroid imbalance.

Can we get too much? Of course. One can have too much of anything. The body is well equipped to deal with too much protein, but too much carbohydrate can result in overweight. There is a considerable safety margin built into our bodies. We can take very large amounts of most substances before they cause damage.

Take copper. We need only a few milligrams a day. But a thousand times that amount, just a few grams, will result in vomiting, and in extreme cases can cause death. Vitamin B_1 can also cause death if it is ingested in amounts ten thousand times the usual daily requirement. Other vitamins in the B-group, however, have never been known to be toxic, regardless of the quantity taken. These include riboflavin and pantothenic acid (B^3).

When an essential nutrient is missing, the healthy individual can go for several days before noticing any ill effects. This is because the body has a certain reserve supply of most essential nutriments, and it will be several days before this supply is exhausted. A slight continuing deficiency may produce no outward signs at all. But the lifespan may be shortened, as certain organs are bound to be affected.

Every cell in the body requires constant nutrition in order to perform its assigned task. If there is too much alcohol present, nutrition will be incomplete, and diseases will appear.

THE CONTROL MECHANISMS

Control mechanisms are the systems that regulate our food intake and excretion. They keep the body in a balanced condition.

For instance, there is a thermostat in our brain. It is very similar in function to the thermostat on your oven. When the body is attacked by a disease, this mechanism is thrown out of sync and body temperature rises and falls abnormally.

There is also a respiratory center in our bodies. This controls our breathing. It is unique in that it can be controlled consciously as well as unconsciously. Ordinarily, the unconscious *autonomic nervous system* controls our breathing reflex by measuring the blood's alkalinity. When this is low, the lung and chest muscles rise, causing us to inhale.

In the case of alcohol and food, we are interested in the appetite mechanism. There are some individuals who never think about their diet or their weight, and who may not vary more than ten pounds one way or the other over a period of twenty years. Considering the many thousands of pounds of food consumed by the average person in twenty years, the sensitivity and exacting control exercised by the appetite mechanism is remarkable.

How this mechanism functions is not clear. We know that it involves the hypothalamus in the brain. This has been clinically proven by experiments that have altered the hypothalamus in test animals. Such altered animals eat vast amounts and become obese.

Hunger is selective. We know that the appetite mechanism frequently calls for the ingestion of specific vitamins and minerals, subject to caloric need, of course. Salt is one of these. When our bodies need salt, we salt our foods heavily and seek out salty foods. Animals show this need all the time. The salt-lick was once a familiar sight in rural areas of the United States. Herbivorous animals do not get sufficient salt in their diets and they will travel miles to a lick.

The parathyroid gland seems to be involved with the appetite for calcium and phosphorous. When this gland is missing or otherwise damaged the calcium level of the blood drops. This results in calcium hunger and an aversion to phosphates. This aversion appears because phosphates have the ability to further deplete available calcium.

The B vitamins can also create specific hungers. It has been found that animals with a B-vitamin deficiency frequently exhibit agitation when given brewer's yeast, a substance rich in certain B vitamins.

What happens when one of the appetite-controlling mechanisms goes out? If the problem is physical, such as a lack of a certain substance because its control mechanism is not working, the missing agent can usually be supplied. For instance, insulin, which is administered to diabetics. If infection is involved, or poisoning, the problem may be resolved by eliminating the poison or treating the infection. If there is a biological problem, if the mechanism functions but on a reduced scale, this can be corrected, too.

Malnutrition is obviously a factor in the working of the control mechanism. This is why they are so closely involved with alcohol abuse. In one study it was found that the appetite mechanism of malnourished children had become disturbed. When given a choice, the children would eat nothing but sugar in spite of an obvious need for other substances. This is a classic example of the effects of a malfunctioning appetite-control mechanism.[1]

The effects of nutrition on an appetite-control mechanism can produce a self-perpetuating eating cycle. When the individual is eating properly, he will continue to do so, making sure that meals are well balanced and nutritious, even when not consciously aware that this is taking place. When the individual is malnourished, his appetite-control mechanism may be damaged to the extent that he consumes large quantities of empty calories in the form of sugar, or alcohol. This, in turn, leads to further malnourishment, which increases the appetite for the empty calories, whatever their source. This leads to further malnutrition.

Now that we know something of how vitamins and minerals and other food substances are used in the body, a brief review is in order.

We know that alcohol is a primary and secondary factor in many diseases and illnesses, most of which are nutritionally based. In addition, heavy alcohol use increases the risk factors in other conditions. The system becomes more susceptible to nonalcohol-related diseases. This leads to a higher mortality rate among those who have drinking problems. Alcoholics can expect their lifespan to be shortened by ten to twelve years.

The liver is the organ most susceptible to damage from alcohol use. This is because it is the site of alcohol metabolism. There is no feedback in the liver and therefore no mechanism to regulate the rate at which alcohol is burned. The metabolism of alcohol produces hydrogen in the liver and causes the accumulation of fat. These fatty materials are then moved into the bloodstream where they create a mild condition known as hyperlipemia.

Alcohol is a factor in the liver degeneration that ultimately leads to alcoholic hepatitis, an inflammation of the liver. Cirrhosis comes about when the liver is scarred and hardened by the direct action of excessive alcohol. This can lead to hemorrhage or liver failure.

Ten per cent of all alcoholics develop cirrhosis, which is the third leading cause of death in New York City.

Alcohol contains many calories, but almost no nutrients. Complications arise when easily digested alcohol replaces other food sources. Nutrients are then unavailable and malnutrition can result.

MORTALITY

Excess drinking affects the death rate primarily through nutritional deficiencies. It is difficult to trace a definite link between alcohol and death as there are so many mitigating factors. People fall into different categories as to type, drinking patterns, physical condition, etc.

The relationship between death and alcohol can be direct or indirect. An example of the first can be seen in the college student who was dared to consume an entire fifth of vodka on an empty stomach. He managed to do it, but he died when alcoholic shock set in. An example of indirect action is an alcohol-induced automobile accident. This comes about because alcohol produces a less than alert mental state. The relationship can also be long term. Cirrhosis can develop for twenty years before it becomes unmanageable.

The study of the relationship between alcohol and mortality began in the last century when researchers tried to discover the amount that could be ingested before disease developed. For the rest of that century and well into our own, various insurance companies undertook studies designed to compare mortality rates of drinkers with nondrinkers. These early studies were in no way conclusive, for they classified everyone according to a preexisting moral concept. The individual who allowed even the tiniest amount of alcohol to touch the lips was considered as hopeless as the chronic alcoholic. So all drinkers were lumped into the same category and no allowances were made for the amounts of alcohol ingested.

After prohibition ended, insurance company studies adopted a two-class comparison. They divided their policyholders into two groups; *standard* and *substandard*. The individuals in the substandard classification are those who are known to be heavy drinkers.

Because of this, we have been given many statistics having to do with mortality rates in heavy drinkers. Comparatively few insurance studies, however, concerned those individuals who are light or social drinkers. Generally speaking, insurance studies indicate that there is a high death rate among those individuals they consider to be substandard.

Several factors should be considered before accepting this conclusion. First, insurance company studies exclude those who do not seek out life insurance. Therefore, many individuals in the lower socio-economic groups and many young people without families who do not feel they need life insurance are not considered. Such studies also do not include those who have been rejected for life insurance. This would naturally exclude many people who are very heavy drinkers and consequently considered uninsurable. Another inconsistency is that those who are considered to be substandard may be so in ways other than drinking.

However, one class study, considered to be a model in general population studies, was conducted in 1926 by Dr. R. Pearl.[19] Dr. Pearl began by dividing his subjects into four classifications.

Moderate occasional. This includes persons who drink any form of alcohol in small amounts. These individuals never become intoxicated and they do not generally drink every day.

Moderate steady. The same standards apply as for moderate occasional except these people drink every day.

Heavy occasional. This would include those who get

drunk occasionally but not regularly. Between periods of excessive intake, these people tend to be abstainers or moderate drinkers.

Heavy steady. This, naturally, includes people who get drunk regularly and frequently.

This system of classification includes drinking frequency as well as quantity drunk.

Dr. Pearl's study provoked controversy when it was published. He found that moderate drinkers exhibited lower mortality rates than abstainers. This would tend to support the study mentioned in our section on *Alcohol and Heart Disease,* which found that alcohol in small quantities is a protective factor in some areas. Among men, Dr. Pearl discovered that *moderate steady* drinkers tend to have a lower mortality rate than *heavy occasional* drinkers. This is true even when the amount of alcohol is the same. In other words, those who go on an occasional binge seem to die earlier than those who drink steadily in moderate amounts.

The results continue to be interesting. They show that among men of all ages, the *moderate steady* drinker exhibits the lowest mortality rate. In older men, the *heavy drinkers* exhibited the lowest mortality rate. This is surprising, but it has considerable support. It seems that heavy drinking is selective in that it kills off weaker drinkers before they advance into old age. So only the hardiest and healthiest *heavy drinkers* age at all.

SUMMARY. General population studies show that the death rate is considerably lower in the general population than it is among persons who drink heavily. This incidence of mortality is dramatic in the case of women and persons in the younger age groups. There is also a considerable amount of evidence supporting an increasing death rate among young drinkers. This is confused, however, by the fact that abstainers have a higher death rate than moderate drinkers.

Mortality rates increase when other external factors

are involved, for instance, smoking. However, age, health and social standing are also important factors.

Figures related to alcohol use are never considered conclusive, mainly due to the variables involved. These include the many ways an alcoholic can die. Suicide frequently occurs among alcoholics. Home accidents happen when the subject is under the influence of alcohol, traffic fatalities and homicides are other variables. The difficulty obviously arises in trying to estimate how much the alcohol itself contributes to an accident. This is impossible to determine unless identical accidents take place with alcohol being a factor in one and not the other.[3]

Generally speaking, the studies cited earlier all indicate that there is a safe amount of alcohol that can be taken without affecting mortality. Beyond that amount, and it varies for every individual, alcohol is definitely a factor in increased mortality rates.

REFERENCES AND ADDITIONAL READING FOR CHAPTER TWO

1. Hillman, R. W., "Alcohol and Malnutrition," *Biology of Alcoholism,* Plenum Press, 1974.
2. McManus, Contag and Olson, *Journal of Biologic Chemistry,* 241, 349, 1966.
3. Brenner, B., "Alcoholism and Fatal Accidents," *Quarterly Journal of Studies in Alcohol,* 28:517-528, 1967.
4. Cahalan, D., Room, R., *Problem Drinking Among American Men,* Monograph No. 7, New Brunswick, New Jersey, Rutgers Center of Alcohol Studies, 1974.
5. Belloc, N., "Relationship of Health Practices and Mortality," *Preventive Medicine,* 2:67-81, 1973.
6. Rushing, W. A., "Alcoholism and Suicide Rates by Status Set and Occupation," *Quarterly Journal of Studies in Alcohol,* 29:399-412, 1968.
7. California State Department of Public Health, *Follow-up Studies of Treated Alcoholics: Mortality,* Division of Alcoholic Rehabilitation, Publication No. 6, Berkeley, California, May, 1961.
8. Jellinek, E. M., "Death from Alcoholism in the United States in 1940. A Statistical Analysis," *Quarterly Journal of Studies in Alcohol,* 3:465-494, 1942.
9. Menge, W. O., "Mortality Experience Among Cases Involving Alcoholic Habits," Proceedings, Home Office Life Underwriters Association, 31:70-93, 1950.
10. Zieve, L., Hill, Earl, "Progression of Classic Signs of Neuropathy and Pellagra During Therapy," *American Journal of Clinical Nutrition,* Vol. 13, November, 1963.
11. Sebrell, W. H., Lowry, J. V., Daft, F. S., Ashburn, L.L., "Polyneuropathy in Thiamin-Deficient Rats Delayed by Alcohol and Whisky," *Journal on Nutrition,* 24:73, 1942.
12. Sebrell, W. H., Jr., Harris, R. S., *The Vitamins,* Vol. 3, Academic Press, New York, 1958.

41

13. Rosenthal, W. S., *et al.,* "Riboflavin Deficiency in Complicated Chronic Alcoholism," *American Journal of Clinical Nutrition.* Vol. 26, August, 1973.

14. Albert, M., LeMay, M., "Denumeralization of the Dorsum Sellae Associated with Alcoholism," *British Journal of Radiology*, 41:331-332.

15. Alexander, C. S., "The Syndrome of Cobalt-Beer Cardiomyopathy Including Infrastructural Changes on Biopsy," *Journal of Laboratory Clinical Medicine,* 72:850, 1969.

16. Arky, R. A., *et al.,* "Irreversible Hypoglycemia: A Complication of Alcohol and Insulin," Journal of the American Medical Association, 206:575-578, 1968.

17. Benjafield, J. G., Rutter, L. F., "Muscle Disease in Chronic Alcoholism," *Lancet,* 1:1292-1293, 1971.

18. Olson, R. E., "Nutrition and Alcoholism," *Modern Nutrition in Health and Disease,* WOHL, 25:767-781, 1970.

19. Pearl, R., *Alcohol and Longevity,* Alfred A. Knopf, New York, 1926.

CHAPTER THREE

THE METABOLISM OF ALCOHOL

While the use of alcohol is a controversial subject, there is general agreement in the scientific community on how the body absorbs and distributes alcohol.

What happens when alcohol enters the body? After it enters the stomach? What effects does alcohol have on the organs of the body? How is it converted into sugar? These are some of the questions we will discuss in this chapter.

Alcohol exhibits none of the expected properties of a food. It doesn't remain in the stomach for any length of time. It is not selectively secreted from the system, nor can it be stored. It does not produce fat. It does not become protein or carbohydrate, and it does not contribute to any other type of tissue. Why then is alcohol considered a food?

Alcohol is a small, neutral, water-soluble molecule. It requires no digestion and frequently enters the system by simple diffusion, that is, it passes directly through the lining of the digestive tract. Also, unlike other foods, which are absorbed in different parts of the digestive system, alcohol can be absorbed anywhere. It passes through the walls of the stomach and rectum just as easily as through the walls of the intestines.

As soon as alcohol enters the stomach, the absorption process begins. Almost 20 per cent passes into the body from the stomach. The other 80 per cent is moved rapidly into the small intestine where it is absorbed almost immediately. It passes into the bloodstream at a rate proportional to its concentration. There seems to be no limit as to the amount of alcohol that can pass through the walls of the gastrointestinal tract. No alcohol whatsoever remains in the intestine. The length of time required for the complete ingestion of alcohol is limited only by the amount of food available in the stomach and by the strength of the solution.

Alcohol can be directly injected into the bloodstream so long as the injection is slow enough not to send a body into shock. It can also be absorbed through the lungs. It is actually possible to inhale enough alcohol to make one drunk. The only part of the body through which it will not readily pass is the skin.

Distribution in the Body: Alcohol is distributed quickly to those organs and tissues that contain large amounts of water. The converse is also true. Bone, for example, contains little water. It does not, therefore, absorb much alcohol. Fat contains relatively small amounts of water due to its poor blood supply. This accounts for the fact that fat people exhibit higher blood concentrations of alcohol than do normal people after the same period of time. Alcohol distribution in other tissues, the brain, for instance, rises and falls with the concentration in the blood.

Alcohol is not excreted in the accepted meaning of the word. Small amounts of it are lost in the urine, and minute quantities are lost through the respiratory system. Most alcohol, once it enters the body, remains there until it is broken down by the liver and its waste products can be expelled.

Different animals metabolize alcohol at different rates, and there is considerable variation within a single species. There are many reasons for this. One is the animal's ability to process protein. The presence of protein in the stomach increases alcohol's metabolic rate, especially the presence of two amino acids, *glycine* and *alanine.*

Fat and carbohydrates have little effect on alcohol, although individuals on high-carbohydrate diets show increased metabolism. Persons on high-fat diets, on the other hand, show a lowered rate. In persons observing a fast, the metabolic rate remains high for the first few days, after which it drops. This drop coincides with the period during which the body is utilizing stored fat reserves. It will increase if the fast is extended to the point where protein reserves are being used.

The metabolic rate does not change with the needs of the individual. Exposure to cold, or muscular exercise, both of which normally increase the body's general metabolism, have no effect on alcohol. Some researchers have reported that *insulin,* an endocrine secretion, and *fructose,* a fruit sugar, both speed up the metabolism of alcohol. However, this is still controversial.[1]

THE PATHWAY OF METABOLISM

The liver and the kidney both produce large quantities of *dehydrogenase,* which is essential in the conversion of alcohol. It is the liver, however, that is most intimately involved with this process. The amount of active liver tissue in the body determines how fast alcohol will be removed from the bloodstream. The kidney has little to do with alcohol metabolism and neither do the lungs, the heart, the muscles and the skin. The brain has no significant alcohol-oxidizing capacity whatsoever.

The Oxidation of Alcohol: When alcohol oxidation takes place in the liver, the alcohol is changed into acetaldehyde by *dehydrogenase,* which contains zinc. The acetaldehyde thus produced is then itself oxidized and turns into acetate.

This process seems to take place at a fixed rate; there is apparently no way to speed it up or slow it down. This is because the alcohol dehydrogenase is easily saturated by relatively small amounts of alcohol and there seems to be a fixed amount of it available. Some researchers go so far as to suggest that the rate of alcohol metabolism is completely independent of the rate at which it enters the body, or of the amount.[1] They find that if this does have an effect it is so small it is scarcely measurable.[2]

Niacin, a B vitamin, is known to have an effect on alcohol metabolism. However, the role it plays is not clear, for there are many factors involved in demonstrating its effect. For instance, before one can prove that a vitamin deficiency can decrease the rate of alcohol metabolism, one would have to be sure that the decrease was not attributable to a lowered food intake.

Many researchers have also tried to discover a connection between a thiamin deficit and decreases in alcohol metabolism. This search has been considerably confused because some alcoholic patients, even those exhibiting extreme vitamin deficiency, are able to metabolize alcohol at least as fast as the normally healthy person. In some cases the alcoholic metabolizes alcohol faster.

There are several studies that show fasting decreases the ability to oxidize alcohol. This is due to a lowering of available alcohol dehydrogenase. One such study was conducted in 1954 by Vitale, Ney and Hegsted. These researchers put adult rats on a weight-losing diet and then measured their ability to metabolize alcohol. While the rats were losing weight, oxidation decreased steadily. When the rats reached a stabilized weight, this ability returned to normal.

THE NUTRITIONAL VALUE OF ALCOHOL

As stated in Chapter One, alcohol is a high-calorie food with no nutritional value. Three ounces of Bourbon, for instance, is the caloric equivalent of about one ounce of fat or oil. Which gives you an idea why alcoholics seem to have so little need for food. And since alcoholic beverages are almost totally deficient in vitamins, minerals and proteins, they can offer nothing but empty calories.[2]

When the calories from alcohol represent only a small percentage of the total caloric intake, they are used in roughly the same way as calories from fats and carbohydrates. But this is not true when alcohol provides the major portion of the day's caloric intake. Such calories do not support growth or restore weight. The reasons for this are not clear. It is possible that alcoholic calories are not useful in any quantity, but when they are available in small amounts this is not detectable. It is also possible that alcohol calories are not utilized properly because of the effect large doses of alcohol have on the skin. When excessive alcohol is present, the blood vessels of the skin dilate, causing the dissipation of heat. Thus, the energy in the alcohol leaves the body before it can be utilized.

There are three deficiency syndromes that are particularly common in alcoholics: nervous disorders resulting from thiamin deficiency; *pellagra,* a niacin deficiency; and *fatty liver,* which is the result of insufficient protein intake. The first two were once thought to be the toxic effects of alcohol itself. We now know that they are the result of vitamin deficiencies and can be remedied by vitamin supplements even if alcohol use remains high.[3]

We eat because we need calories, not because we

need any particular vitamin or mineral. When this calorie need is fulfilled, the appetite decreases accordingly. Alcohol is almost unique in its ability to supply calories which will satisfy the appetite without supplying vitamins and minerals as well. This is why the heavy drinker so often endangers his health by not eating properly.

REFERENCES AND ADDITIONAL READING FOR CHAPTER THREE

1. Pawan, G. L. S., "Metabolism of Alcohol (Ethanol) in Man," *Procedures of the Nutritional Society,* 31, 83, 1972.
2. Westerfield, W. W., Schulman, M. P., "Metabolism and Caloric Value of Alcohol," *Journal of the American Medical Association,* Vol. 170, No. 2, May 9, 1959.
3. Gordon, E. S., *Nutritional and Vitamin Therapy in General Practice,* Year Book Publishers, Chicago, Illinois, 1947.

CHAPTER FOUR

ALCOHOL'S EFFECTS ON METABOLISM

PROTEIN METABOLISM

Alcoholics are almost always protein deficient. This can partly be explained by alcohol's appetite-depressing ability. It is complicated by what seems to be a connection between a lack of protein in the diet and food intake. Experimental animals fed on low-protein diets have been seen to eat less and less in spite of the caloric content of their food. So, it would seem that excessive alcoholic intake has a far greater effect on protein than it does on other nutritional factors.

The reason for this is not clear. Some researchers have hypothesized that a low-protein diet may have a depressing effect on the enzymes needed to process alcohol, particularly dehydrogenase.[1] There is substantial evidence in support of this. In 1953 Kerner and Westerfield conducted an experiment on rats. It was found that very young rats have almost no ability to deal with alcohol. After being fed on a regular diet for approximately two weeks, however, it was found that this ability increased to the same level as that of adult animals. Presumably this is due to the commencement of alcohol dehydrogenase production.

In further support of this hypothesis, young and adult rats were fed for a time on low-protein diets. The ability of the rats' livers to oxidize alcohol dropped 85 per cent. Complete starvation also had this effect but to a lesser degree. This seems to uphold the theory that low-protein diets limit the production of alcohol dehydrogenase.[2]

It would seem then, that the ability to oxidize alcohol is in direct proportion to the amount of protein in the diet. It then becomes important to know which proteins stimulate the production of dehydrogenase. Researchers have found that milk and egg protein are the most effective. It has also been learned that a *well-balanced diet* in which two-thirds of the protein is derived from vegetable sources is also highly effective (more so than protein *solely* derived from such sources).

There is, however, an inconsistency in the results of this study. While milk was found to be just as effective as eggs or a balanced diet in preventing death from alcohol poisoning, at the same time, it was found that milk is considerably less effective at preventing intoxication than are either of the other two protein sources. This might be due to the varying effects different types of protein have on the absorption rate of alcohol. This has been supported by later experiments. It was found that the average alcohol level in rats fed on milk powder was almost double that found in rats fed on egg powder or mixed foods.[8]

There can be no doubt that alcohol has considerable effect on protein metabolism. Other research has confirmed that it effects the *digestion* of proteins; the amino acids, which are the form of protein that the body utilizes; the movement of these amino acids in the blood; and their use in the body's cells. It also has a depressing effect on general protein synthesis.

Digestion: Small amounts of alcohol can have a favorable effect on the appetite and digestion. Exactly why this is so is not clear. Some researchers suggest that perhaps alcohol stimulates the taste buds. It has also been suggested that due to alcohol's ability to create a feeling of contentment and mellowness, there might be some sort of lubricating effect upon the appetite mechanism.

Alcohol in small quantities stimulates the secretion of gastric juices regardless of the method used to introduce it into the system. It could be breathed in through the lungs and the gastric juices would flow. Alcohol also increases the secretion of pancreatic juices but only if it is taken in through the mouth.

The reader will note that these processes are stimulated by *small* amounts of alcohol. When dealing with excessive amounts, the situation is reversed. Alcoholics almost always evidence severely reduced rates of gastric secretion. Again, this directly affects protein digestion.

Pepsin and *trypsin* are enzymes used in the digestion of protein. They are secreted in the stomach. It has been discovered that small amounts of alcohol, a 5 to 7 per cent solution, for example, slightly inhibits the action of pepsin, while a three per cent solution slightly inhibits the action of trypsin. A concentration of 20 per cent alcohol completely halts the actions of these enzymes. It is, therefore, fortunate that alcohol passes through the stomach so quickly. If it is more or less constantly present, a situation could arise in which protein digestion would be completely halted. Naturally, this happens only in extreme cases of chronic alcoholism.[8]

Absorption of Protein: In order for the body to use protein, it must first be broken down into amino acids. These acids then pass through the intestinal walls and nourish the various tissues. Researchers have reported that relatively low concentrations of alcohol can inhibit these substances, preventing them from passing through the intestinal walls. This inhibition comes about when solutions of from 4 per cent to 19 per cent alcohol are present. Naturally, the amount of inhibition is in direct proportion to strength of the solution. Over 19 per cent, alcohol can almost totally depress amino acid absorption.

It should be noted, however, that the depression of amino acids seems to be quite selective. Some are not affected at all. Some are slowed, particularly those normally absorbed very rapidly. Others are less affected. Still others are absorbed more rapidly than normal.

The intestine is not the only site where amino acid absorption is inhibited. The liver is also affected. This could almost be made a general rule; the liver, the organ that deals with alcohol, is profoundly affected by almost any concentration.[8]

It may seem to some that the alcohol concentrations needed to inhibit amino acid absorption are too high to cause general concern. However, they are no higher than concentrations generally present in the system of a normal person after drinking heavily.

Amino Acids in the Blood: There is evidence that alcohol has considerable effect on the level of free amino acids in the blood. In 1964 an experiment was conducted by Dr. Siegel and his associates using volunteers from Alcoholics Anonymous and patients from the alcoholic wards of hospitals. These men and women were studied and compared to members of a control group of healthy people who were moderate drinkers. The blood of the two groups was first analyzed for free amino acids. The first group, which we will refer to as the alcoholic group, showed an increased level of some amino acids and a depressed level of others.

The blood alcohol levels of the control group were then raised and a comparison was made with the blood of alcoholics taken upon admission to a hospital. In the control group there was a marked depression of 5 amino acids. In the alcoholic group, only one was depressed, whereas other amino acids remained the same or actually increased. The only increase seen in the control group was in levels of the amino acid *glutamine*. There was no change in the level of this acid among the alcoholic subjects.

Glucose Production: The body generally finds glucose in carbohydrates. However, whenever conditions exist that prevent adequate amounts of glucose from being available, particularly in the brain, which feeds entirely on sugars, glucose is manufactured from other substances. One of these is protein.

Many researchers have shown that blood sugar is lowered after the ingestion of alcohol. Some studies also indicate that the body's ability to synthesize sugar from noncarbohydrate sources is seriously impaired. One study was conducted on a group of starving men. It was discovered that increases in blood sugar, appearing after the injection of various amino acids, were totally blocked by the simultaneous administration of alcohol.[3]

There is some support for the contention that the movement of amino acids into the cells may be directly blocked by alcohol. But other researchers have shown that it is the end products of alcohol oxidation that inhibit the utilization and availability of precursors for sugar synthesis. A precursor is a building block for another substance.[3]

Biosynthesis of Protein Tissue: We have seen that alcohol profoundly affects the absorption, transport and use of protein. There is evidence that alcohol must also affect protein synthesis.

In 1959 Dr. Quastel proved that very small concentrations of alcohol can greatly slow the absorption of *glycine,* the simplest amino acid, into tissue. Protein synthesis is dependent on a substance known as ATP, and ATP is not formed unless amino acids are present. Dr. Quastel showed that alcohol inhibits ATP, and thus, protein synthesis.

The pancreas is also active in tissue synthesis. Current research concerns the effect of prolonged alcoholic consumption on protein synthesis in this gland. These studies concern the synthesis of trypsin, the stomach enzyme mentioned earlier, as well as total protein. In one experiment, rats were fed a balanced diet but were given only a 20 per cent alcohol solution to drink. Protein levels were then monitored. It was found that pancreatic protein synthesis was severely depressed. Since the food intake of these animals was carefully controlled, it was obvious that this decrease was a direct result of the presence of alcohol.[8]

Summary: We have seen the effects of alcohol on the body. It decreases absorption of outside protein. It slows or prevents protein utilization due to its effect on the enzymes normally associated with protein digestion. And alcohol seriously impairs protein synthesis.

MINERAL METABOLISM

Excessive amounts of alcohol also affect mineral metabolism. There are two reasons for this. First, alcohol greatly increases the excretion rate of some minerals, preventing their proper utilization. These minerals include zinc, magnesium and calcium. Second, alcohol depresses the appetite, so that sufficient amounts of minerals are not available to the body. Potassium deficiency generally comes about in this manner. In addition, diarrhea and vomiting cause complications by removing minerals before the body has an opportunity to use them.

Magnesium: Magnesium deficiency is one of the most serious complications of alcoholism. This mineral is highly concentrated in the cells and is absolutely essential to the proper maintenance of the skeletal structure. It is also an important component of intracellular fluids as it is an activator of many of the body's enzymes.

Magnesium is particularly vital in the activation of ATP, which is essential in protein synthesis. Magnesium is therefore vitally important in keeping the body going. Magnesium is also important to muscle contraction, secretion, cell activity and all other energy-dependent processes. It is also vital to energy transfer, energy storage, and to the utilization of food substances. It is also a stabilizer for the important DNA and RNA molecules that are responsible for carrying and implementing the important genetic codes. In short, magnesium is essential to life.

Magnesium deficiency promotes widespread deficiencies of other substances. It exacerbates thiamin deficiency and prevents resumption of biochemical activity even after this is corrected. The magnesium must also be replaced before normal biochemical activity can resume. Various researchers have demonstrated that alcohol ingestion affects the secretion of both calcium and magnesium.[9]

Comparatively few studies have been conducted concerning magnesium decrease and its effect on heart and muscle tissue. During the inquiry into the cobalt deaths discussed earlier, the heart tissue of several of the dying patients were examined. It was noted that it contained significantly less magnesium than that of similar patients who were not alcoholics.[10]

There is a striking similarity between the symptoms exhibited by chronic alcoholics as they withdraw from alcohol and the symptoms of magnesium deficiency. Alcohol withdrawal is characterized by restlessness, hyperventilation, tremors, convulsions, bizarre movements, confusion and disorientation. Auditory and visual hallucinations also occur. Magnesium deficiency also causes tremors as well as twitching, bizarre movements, and auditory and visual hallucinations. This similarity is quite intriguing, although there is no conclusive proof yet that a relationship exists.[9]

While there is general agreement that magnesium deficiency is connected with chronic alcoholism, there is considerable disagreement about the role magnesium plays in such severe manifestations as *delirium tremens*.

Zinc: Zinc is a trace element. It is present only in minute quantities. The need for zinc has been proven beyond doubt, although the amounts required are still open to conjecture. Zinc is found in many substances in the body, including a number of enzymes. It is also found in insulin but does not seem to be a factor in the activity of the chemical. It is present in high concentrations in the retina of the eye, in the testicles, and in brain and bone tissue. Zinc is also known to be necessary for RNA metabolism as well as for DNA synthesis.[11]

Exactly how zinc acts in the system is still controversial. We know it is vital in the growth process, particularly in the sexual maturation of the male. This was confirmed in 1963 by a study conducted by Dr. Prasad and his associates on male adolescents. They found that zinc deficiency results in dwarfism and sexual immaturity. Zinc therapy, however, seems to be quite effective in correcting these problems. How a zinc deficiency might affect adults still is not known.

In 1959 studies were first undertaken by Vallee and his associates to prove the relationship, or lack of it, between zinc metabolism and chronic alcoholism. It was found that the livers of alcoholics lack zinc, as does their blood plasma. Later studies revealed that concentrations of zinc in red blood cells is severely reduced in alcoholics. How this affects the body is not known. However, it is clear that many enzymes dealing with DNA synthesis and RNA metabolism require zinc. These are vital in the growth and repair of the liver.[11]

Again, it is the abusive dietary habits of heavy drinkers that contributes to the problem of zinc deficiency. The condition can be corrected, however, by the implementation of a balanced diet.

Calcium: In 1963 Dr. Kalbfleish and his associates demonstrated that there is a two-fold increase in calcium excretion after the intake of alcohol. This supported a study conducted in 1959 on chronic alcoholics that found lowered blood-calcium levels in six out of thirty patients.[12]

In 1969 Dr. Estep and his associates conducted a study that has contributed significantly to our knowledge of magnesium and calcium deficiencies in chronic alcoholics, particularly during the withdrawal period. Twenty-one patients with lowered calcium levels were studied. The bone tissue of these subjects appeared to be normal. Six received no special treatment other than an adequate diet accompanied by multivitamin supplements.

Ordinarily this kind of calcium deficiency indicates some sort of parathyroid deficiency. Thirteen of these men were therefore treated with parathyroid extract, or PTE. In five of the thirteen, calcium levels rose. The other eight patients, however, did not respond satisfactorily to the treatment. This led to the conclusion that the difficulty had to be connected to the reduced magnesium levels that accompanied the calcium deficiency, rather than to a specific parathyroid difficulty. The experiment was repeated, this time after magnesium had been replaced by intravenous injection. The response to the PTE was entirely normal in every respect.

The following conclusions were drawn: low calcium levels are due to a temporary lack of response to PTE; and this lack of response is due to magnesium deficiency. Thus, the thyroid's dependence on magnesium, and calcium's on magnesium, was clearly demonstrated.

Another disease frequently found in alcoholics is *osteoporosis*. This is degeneration of bone tissue associated with a calcium deficiency. The exact cause of the disease in alcoholics is not clear. Possibly, the increased calcium excretion caused by alcohol depletes the calcium supply to such an extent that it affects the bone tissue. Malnutrition could also be the cause.[12]

Potassium: Potassium excretion also increases after alcohol ingestion. Therefore, alcoholics frequently exhibit potassium deficiency. In one study on fifty alcoholic patients, 46 per cent were moderately depleted and 18 per cent were severely depleted. These last patients also exhibited vomiting and diarrhea, while seventy-six of the patients exhibited heart irregularities.[12]

Potassium deficiency is difficult to diagnose. Identical symptoms can be caused by a number of problems. These symptoms include muscle weakness, sometimes to the point of paralysis, and abnormal heart rhythms. This makes treatment for heart irregularities difficult, for one of the standard treatments is the administration of glucose without additional potassium; this lowers potassium levels. So, if the heart irregularity is due to lack of potassium, a treatment that lowers potassium levels still further can be dangerous.

Mineral poisoning: Mineral poisoning sometimes occurs when metals are accidentally ingested with alcohol. An excellent example of this is the cobalt poisoning discussed earlier. After it became clear that cobalt was responsible for the deaths, cobalt-induced heart damage began to be recognized as an entity unto itself. Studies were begun and several conclusions were reached.

First, many doctors prescribe medicines containing cobalt for their patients without any particular damage resulting. It is also significant that many thousands of people drank the contaminated beers and only a few of these suffered ill effects. This indicates that cobalt itself is not the problem. The complications must have arisen from some other difficulty that interacted with the cobalt, causing the deaths. There is evidence that cobalt is rendered harmless by protein. Therefore, a diet rich in protein would protect one against cobalt poisoning. If the alcoholics who died had been eating normally their deaths would probably not have occurred.[12]

In 1968 Hall and Smith conducted an experiment on rabbits. The animals were injected with cobalt chloride. Some died of heart failure and all exhibited heart tissue degeneration quite similar to that found in the hearts of the cobalt/beer drinkers.

Also in 1968 a researcher named Sullivan did a study on the hearts of a number of the cobalt-poisoned patients in Omaha, Nebraska. Not only did the hearts of these patients evidence extremely high level of cobalt, but their magnesium, zinc and manganese levels were all significantly lower than would have been expected in the hearts of normal patients.[10]

Thankfully, the FDA has outlawed the use of cobalt in beer and the danger has passed.

Lead poisoning is also frequently associated with alcohol, particularly in the case of drinkers of moonshine whisky. The stills used by moonshiners are often no more than old car radiators, which contain large amounts of lead in the metal work. Alcohol picks up this lead and moonshine users ingest it along with the whisky. The use of lead pipe is also a factor. It is interesting to note that lead poisoning was not considered the cause of death among moonshine alcoholics for a long time because the symptoms were hidden among all the other factors complicating alcoholism.[12]

There are two types of lead poisoning: acute and chronic. Chronic poisoning is associated with a long-term exposure to lead, but it shares many characteristics with the acute form. Common symptoms include anemia, with attendant weakness, insomnia, headache, dizziness and irritability. It can also be identified, in patients who do not brush their teeth by a black line at the base of the teeth caused by deposits of lead sulfide. Acute lead poisoning can cause brain damage, blindness and death.

VITAMIN METABOLISM

The question of vitamin metabolism in relation to alcohol is extremely complex. This is because alcohol, as a carbohydrate food, makes demands upon the body that require the utilization of vitamin substances. But alcohol also prevents the proper utilization of many vitamins, making it the chief cause of vitamin deficiency among alcoholics who do not maintain adequate food intake.

Some alcoholics may exhibit normal vitamin levels if they have not progressed to the point where their drinking has begun to interfere with eating. In cases where this has already begun, the individual is almost certain to show vitamin deficiencies. This is also complicated by the development of vitamin-depletion syndromes directly attributable to defects in the intestinal vitamin-absorption mechanism, or to an increasing inability to convert vitamins into biologically active forms.

Food Intake: It is always difficult to get any kind of a comprehensive history of food consumption when dealing with alcoholics. So many factors come into play —religious background, economic and ethnic status— that it is difficult to separate them from altered eating habits.

As a general rule it is safe to say that heavy consumption of alcohol leads to a marked change in eating habits because alcohol itself provides so many calories. This has been given support by a recent study conducted among three thousand alcoholic patients in a large metropolitan hospital. It was found that 40 per cent of these patients exhibited vitamin deficiency during periods of heavy drinking. In addition, 25 per cent of these patients exhibited deficiencies even when their drinking alternated with periods of normal eating. Fully

35 per cent exhibited constant deficiency except when they were hospitalized.[7]

Vitamin Needs in Alcohol Metabolism: In order for alcohol to be properly oxidized, there must be a functioning electron transport system. This system must be supplied with nicotinic acid and riboflavin, both essential vitamins. If either of these substances is absent or decreased the removal of alcohol from the system is slowed. In addition, continuous alcohol intake requires increased amounts of thiamin, biotin and vitamin B_6 in order that certain enzymes can react properly.

Vitamins are also needed in the repair of alcohol-damaged tissue. Ascorbic acid (vitamin C) is needed in *collagen* synthesis. Collagen is the basic building material of all muscle tissue and is therefore vital in tissue repair. Cell replacement is dependent on folic acid, B_{12} and vitamin B_6. If folic acid and vitamin B_{12} are not available, DNA synthesis will be impared, in both the liver and in the bone marrow. If B_6 is missing, a significant reduction in protein and nucleic-acid synthesis will result.

Vitamin Absorption Problems: In alcoholics with intestinal disease, liver disease and disease of the pancreas, a decrease in absorption of certain fat-soluble vitamins is often seen. Water-soluble vitamins are also affected but to a lesser degree. Thiamin is particularly susceptible in this case, a fact that has been supported by studies in which alcohol is ingested prior to thiamin injection. Forty to 60 per cent of the body's ability to absorb thiamin is impaired by alcohol. However, the question of thiamin retention and absorption related to alcohol is controversial and will be dealt with more fully later in this section.

Alcohol affects vitamin absorption regardless of how it enters the body. In normal healthy persons who eat regularly and drink infrequently the effects of this are not severe and are short lived. In people showing symptoms of malnourishment, such as fatty liver, proper vitamin absorption will not begin again until the entire body is healthy.

Vitamin Storage: Normally, vitamins are stored in the body. In the normal individual, there is enough of a backlog to allow several weeks of depletion before the onset of adverse effects. This is why the occasional drinker generally remains healthy, even when such drinking is carried to excess. Most vitamins are stored almost indiscriminately in the liver. This is because the liver stores vitamins depending upon how many are available, not upon how many are needed. Alcoholics with liver damage frequently evidence a lack of vitamin storage capability.

Symptoms of Vitamin Deficiency: Many of the symptoms of alcoholism can be directly attributed to vitamin deficiency. These include anemia, glossitis, and neuritis. Liver, neuropsychiatric and heart lesions may also occur. A fatty liver condition is further aggravated by a deficiency of nicotinic acid and riboflavin.

There is no conclusive evidence that delirium tremens, the ultimate alcoholic disturbance, is connected with vitamin deficiency. Even though there is a dramatic decrease in hallucinations and nervousness after the administration of thiamin, nicotinic acid and vitamin B_6, these vitamins do nothing to hasten recovery after delirium tremens. There is some evidence that inadequate utilization of some vitamins aggravates this condition. This is supported by what is known of the slowing of brain-tissue oxidation during attacks of delirium tremens. It may also explain the occasional abnormal behavior exhibited by alcoholics.

The relationship between heart disease and alcohol needs more study before any conclusions can be made.

Thiamin: Thiamin has been mentioned frequently throughout this book. That is because thiamin and folic acid are the two most important vitamins to consider when discussing alcohol. There is a direct connection between thiamin deficiency and alcoholism. However, no researcher has as yet been able to say exactly what it is. Naturally, thiamin deficiency varies from individual to individual and there are many factors contributing to the problem.

The first factor to be considered is decreased dietary intake. Naturally, if the body is taking in less thiamin than it needs, it will show a deficiency.

Another contributing factor might be a change in the body's ability to absorb thiamin. This has been supported by several studies. In 1968 Thomassulo, Kater and Iber conducted an experiment in which they administered a fixed amount of thiamin to two different groups of patients. The first group were hospitalized alcoholics. The second, also hospitalized, was not alcoholic. The results of this study proved that alcoholics are not able to absorb thiamin as efficiently as non-alcoholics. After initial measurements were taken, the alcoholic subjects were fed on balanced diets with no alcohol for two and a half months. It was found that their ability to absorb thiamin had returned to normal. A similar experiment was conducted on animals by another group in 1968 with the same results.[6]

There is also considerable evidence that alcoholic liver injury affects the individual's ability to deal with thiamin, even when it is being administered in treatment. In 1969 Cole and his associates were able to show that there is a definite relationship between the state of the liver and the body's ability to respond to thiamin. Earlier in this chapter, we learned of the importance of magnesium to bodily processes. It has been proved that magnesium and thiamin are closely related by the response of subjects exhibiting both thiamin and magnesium deficiencies. They respond differently to thiamin treatment than do subjects lacking only thiamin.

In 1969 research was carried out in order to more clearly define the relationship of thiamin deficiency to magnesium deficiency. Again, rats were used. One group was given alcohol in drinking water in addition

65

to being made thiamin/magnesium deficient. A second group was made thiamin/magnesium deficient but given no alcohol. The diets of both groups were carefully regulated to create differing amounts of deficiency as well as different combinations of thiamin and magnesium. The study concluded that magnesium deficiency causes the body to respond poorly to thiamin treatment. An inconsistancy appeared, however, in that both the alcoholic and nonalcoholic groups reacted in precisely the same way. In addition, the alcoholic rats exhibited an *increased* ability to withstand the thiamin deficiency. Why this inconsistency exists is still being studied.[4]

The liver's ability to store vitamins is adversely affected by alcohol-related damage and disease. Next to insufficient dietary intake, this is probably the greatest cause of vitamin deficiency in alcoholics. It accounts for a lack of folic acid and pyridoxine (vitamin B_6) as well as a lack of thiamin. Indeed, these deficiencies have frequently been noted in patients suffering from fatty liver and cirrhosis. Again, there is no definite proof, at this time, that alcohol affects the retention of these vitamins. Most available evidence, however, seems to point in that direction.

Folic Acid: Folic acid is another vitamin deficient in alcoholics, especially those with liver disease. It is a water-soluble vitamin obtained from fresh, green, leafy vegetables and fruit, as well as from organ meats such as liver.

In 1955 Klipstein and Lindenbaum began a study with fifty-five alcoholics exhibiting varying degrees of liver disease. Nineteen of these subjects exhibited a folic acid deficiency due to insufficient dietary intake. Among the other subjects there was no evidence of folic acid deficiency whenever dietary intake could be considered adequate. This study was unable to find any definite connection between liver disease and folic acid deficiency.

As a result of this study, researchers believed for quite some time that folic acid deficiency and liver damage were not connected. However, in 1965, another view was advanced by Dr. Cherrick and his associates. A radioactive type of folic acid was administered to six patients suffering from severe cirrhosis of the liver and six other subjects with no liver damage. At the outset, none of the twelve subjects exhibited any signs of folic acid deficiency. Excretion of the radioactive form of the vitamin in the alcoholic patients was approximately ten times that evidenced by the nonalcoholics. Dr. Cherrick therefore concluded that liver damage is a definite factor in folic acid deficiency.

We have two conflicting opinions, the second supported to a considerable degree by the fact that folic acid deficiency seems to run hand in hand with thiamin deficiency and that both seem to be present in alcoholics. What can be the reason for this? Could it be that *absorption* of folic acid is affected by alcohol consumption?

In 1967 Halsted, Griggs and Harris studied a group of twenty-three subjects hospitalized because of prolonged drinking bouts. None of these men had been drinking less than three weeks. They were divided into two groups: the first group was composed of individuals who had been drinking within forty-eight hours of the beginning of the study; members of the second group had not been drinking for at least a week. All of these subjects were dosed with radioactive folic acid and the levels of the vitamin in their blood were then analyzed. Members of the first group exhibited significantly less folic acid in their blood than either members of the second group or members of a control group of healthy persons. As a final test, the researchers administered alcohol to a group of volunteers who were not heavy drinkers and then compared the results. It was found that folic acid absorption was completely unimpaired in the nonalcoholic volunteers. It was concluded, therefore, that continued intake of large amounts of alcohol is a factor in creating folic acid deficiency.

Other researchers have continued to work in this field. One group studied the effect of folic acid in moderate amounts on alcoholics. They learned that folic acid in the amount prescribed as the minimum daily requirement is totally suppressed by the concurrent consumption of large amounts of alcohol. The only way that the folic could have any effect in this case was to increase the dosages considerably—or eliminate the alcohol.[13]

Vitamin A: Vitamin A, or *Retinol*, is a fat-soluble vitamin found in fish, oils, liver, egg yolks, butter, cream, and leafy green or yellow vegetables. It is dangerous in extremely large quantities. Experiments conducted on dogs and rats indicate that vitamin A levels in the blood *rise* after the administration of alcohol, which could be a danger.[5]

This rise in vitamin A levels after alcohol ingestion raises some intriguing questions. Does the alcohol act directly on vitamin-A-bearing tissues in the body and thus cause it to be released into the blood? Or does the alcohol act on some other mechanism which, in turn, causes this rise? This last possibility has found a certain amount of support. It has been found, for instance, that certain of the adrenal hormones, when injected into the body, cause an increase in Retinol. It is also known that alcohol stimulates the adrenal glands. It is possible, therefore, that the mobilization of vitamin A by alcohol is due to the action of the adrenal hormones. Later studies have shown, however, that direct stimulation is more likely to be the answer.

Vitamin A, like so many other vitamins, is stored in the liver. There is evidence to support the contention that alcohol releases vitamin A into the blood by directly mobilizing this liver store. Researchers have demonstrated that prolonged alcohol ingestion reduces the amount of available vitamin A in the livers of rats and chickens. In 1965 a report was published by Melvin Lee and S. P. Lucia that gave definite proof that vitamin A in the liver is directly mobilized by alcohol.[5]

This study was performed using dogs. The adrenal glands were removed from some dogs while the pancreas was removed from others. Alcohol was then administered directly into the veins. All of the dogs evidenced a rise in vitamin A. The conclusion? That alcohol acts directly on the liver, stimulating it to release quantities of vitamin A into the blood.[5]

There are, of course, many other vitamins to be considered when one wishes to maintain good health. It would not serve our purpose, however, to continue with descriptions of studies of all the other vitamins, especially as it is clear that alcohol does effect the metabolism, absorption and utilization of the vitamins already mentioned. This seems to be a general rule rather than an exception. Let us now move into the area of carbohydrates.

CARBOHYDRATE METABOLISM

It has been observed for many years that alcoholics are subject to hypoglycemia, or low blood sugar. This is apparently due to the interference of alcohol with the normal conversion of carbohydrates into sugar. It should be remembered that alcohol is a carbohydrate and a particularly convenient calorie. It does not have to be digested and can be directly utilized by the body. It therefore replaces other forms of carbohydrates and makes them unnecessary in filling the daily caloric need. These excess carbohydrates are then stored — creating fat in the case of the alcoholic who maintains adequate food intake.

In only one area do alcoholic beverages offer any nutritional value. Malt liquors and wines contain particles of unfermented grains and fruit that can supply some nutriments. The carbohydrate content of malt liquors, not including the carbohydrate found in the alcohol itself, is approximately 3 to 6 per cent. That of wine varies, with the dry wines containing 1 to 4 per cent carbohydrate, and the sweet wines containing as much as 20 percent. In some cases, the carbohydrate content of the beverages might supply some of the daily requirement. In addition, some malt beverages furnish small amounts of B-complex vitamins. These actually serve to stimulate the appetite rather than diminish it, as do the stronger alcoholic beverages. This is felt to be the main factor in the weight increases seen in many individuals who consume large quantities of beer.

Summary: The effect of alcohol consumption on the body's metabolic systems is controversial. This controversy arises not from discussion as to whether or not alcohol is harmful, but from disagreement as to exactly why alcohol causes so many adverse reactions.

In the next chapter we will examine alcohol's effects on such vital systems as the heart, the brain and the central nervous system.

ALCOHOL'S EFFECTS ON METABOLISM

REFERENCES AND ADDITIONAL READING FOR CHAPTER FOUR

1. Tremolieres, J., Lowy, R., Griffaton, G., "Metabolic Effects of Ethanol," *Procedures of the Nutritional Society,* 31, 107, 1972.
2. Westerfield, W. W., Kerner, E., *Procedures of the Society for Experimental and Biological Medicine,* 83, 530-32, 1953.
3. Fry, M. M., *et al.,* "Intensification of Hypertriglyceridemia by Either Alcohol or Carbohydrate," *American Journal on Clinical Nutrition,* Vol. 26, No. 8, August, 1973.
4. Vitale, J. J., Coffey, J., "Alcohol and Vitamin Metabolism," *Biology of Alcoholism,* Vol. 1, 1970.
5. Lee, M., Lucia, S. P., "Effect of Ethanol on the Mobilization of Vitamin A in the Dog and Rat," *Quarterly Journal on the Study of Alcohol,* Vol. 26, No. 1, March, 1965.
6. Senter, R. J., Sinclair, J. D., "Thiamin-Induced Alcohol Consumption in Rats," *Quarterly Journal on the Study of Alcohol,* Vol. 29, No. 2, June, 1968.
7. "Vitamins and Alcoholism," *American Journal on Clinical Nutrition,* Vol. 21, 1325-28, 1968.
8. Orten, J. M., Sardesai, V. M., "Interrelationship Between Protein and Alcohol Metabolism," *Biology of Alcoholism,* Vol. 1, Chapter 7.
9. Sullivan, J. F., *et al.,* "Magnesium Metabolism in Alcoholism," *American Journal on Clinical Nutrition,* Vol. 13, November, 1963.
10. Sullivan, J. F., *et al.,* "Myocardiopathy of Beer Drinkers: Subsequent Course," *Annual of Internal Medicine,* 1968.
11. Sullivan, J. F., Lankford, N. G., "Zinc Metabolism and Chronic Alcoholism," *American Journal on Clinical Nutrition,* Vol. 17, No. 2, August, 1965.
12. Flink, E. B., "Mineral Metabolism in Alcoholism," *Biology of Alcoholism,* Vol. 1, 1970.

71

13. Sullivan, J. F., *et al.*, "Folic Acid Metabolism in Alcoholics," *American Journal on Clinical Nutrition*, 1964.
14. Best, C. H., *et al.*, *British Medical Journal*, II, 1001-6, 1949.
15. Lester, D., *Quarterly Journal on the Study of Alcohol*, 22, 554-74, 1961.
16. Rosenthal, W. S., *et al.*, "Riboflavin Deficiency in Complicated Chronic Alcoholism," *American Journal on Clinical Nutrition*, Vol. 26, No. 8, August, 1973.
17. Arky, R. A., "Influences of Alcohol on the Anabolic Phase of Carbohydrate Metabolism," *Biology of Alcoholism*, Vol. 1, No. 6, 198-221.
18. Morley, N. H., Clarke, D. W., "Influence of Ethanol and Tolbutamide on Carbohydrate Metabolism in the Dog," *Quarterly Journal of the Study of Alcoholism*, Vol. 28, No. 4; December, 1967.
19. O'Keane, M., *et al.*, "Ascorbic Acid Status of Alcoholics," *Journal of Alcoholism*, Vol. 7, No. 1, 1972.
20. Badawy, A., Evans, M., "Alcohol and Tryptophan Metabolism," *Journal of Alcoholism*, Vol. 9, No. 3, 1974.
21. Leevy, C. M., *et al.*, "B-Complex Vitamins in Liver Disease of the Alcoholic." *American Journal on Clinical Nutrition*, Vol. 1, No. 4, April, 1965.
22. Blackstock, E. E., *et al.*, "The Role of Thiamin Deficiency in the Aetiology of the Hallucinatory States Complicating Alcoholism," *British Journal of Psychiatry*, 121, 357-64, 1972.

CHAPTER FIVE

ALCOHOL: Its Effect on the Vital Systems

THE HEART

It is no secret that heart disease is the leading cause of death in the United States. This fact is mentioned constantly in magazines, on the radio and on television. There are always drives being conducted for funds to aid in the research which, it is hoped, will help bring about better understanding of heart disease. What about alcohol and the heart? For many years it was felt that alcohol had little direct effect on coronary heart disease. Recent evidence, however, has caused researchers to become more concerned about the toxic effects of alcohol and how they might apply to this problem.

Several avenues of research seem to be presenting contradictory evidence. In one instance it has been indicated that alcohol is not an important factor in coronary heart disease.[18] Most of this evidence has been provided by autopsies performed on alcoholics. Some researchers have also found that small amounts of alcohol in nonalcoholic individuals seem to lower heart-attack risk.[19]

In the second instance recent studies have found that alcohol is a factor in *cardiomyopathy,* a disease of the heart muscle. (Coronary heart disease is associated with the blood vessels rather than with the muscle.) These studies indicate that even moderate amounts of alcohol might weaken the heart muscle itself.[20]

Cardiomyopathy is definitely a factor in the deaths of many alcoholics. This has been verified many times, even in cases where malnutrition is not concerned. In view of this evidence, the disease has been renamed *alcoholic cardiomyopathy,* in spite of the fact that the mechanism that causes the disease still eludes us.

The medical community is sharply divided as to whether or not alcohol is a factor in this disease. This is surprising in that coronary heart disease and alcoholic cardiomyopathy are two completely different problems. It is quite possible that alcohol could be beneficial in one case and detrimental in the other. In spite of this, the controversy continues.

Alcoholic Cardiomyopathy: Cardiomyopathy is a distinct entity. A heart appears large and flabby when this disease is present. But the valves of the heart look entirely normal and there is little material inside the arteries and vessels that could be considered significant. Recent examinations of hearts that have been affected by this disease, using the latest electron microscopes, show that the tissue of the heart is remarkably similar to that seen in alcohol-damaged livers.[12]

Recently, a study was undertaken in which an alcoholic individual received a balanced diet for six months. This diet was regularly supplemented with vitamins and minerals. In spite of this, when alcohol was administered, the patient exhibited all of the symptoms of cardiomyopathy. These symptoms vanished when the alcohol was discontinued.

In another experiment in which rats were fed an

adequate diet in concert with regular amounts of alcohol, their hearts became fatty and enlarged. Over a period of months, the heart function of these rats decreased considerably. When studied under the electron microscope, the heart tissue was identical with that seen in the hearts of human beings who had died of the disease.

Exactly how the heart muscle is affected by alcohol is unclear. It is possible that the heart is attacked directly. It is equally possible that the alcohol stimulates some part of the body to produce some substance which then attacks the heart. More research is necessary before we understand the connection.

In the meantime treatment for this disease consists almost entirely of bed rest and abstinence. If treatment is begun in time, the patient usually recovers. Unfortunately, as in other diseases, many patients evidence irreversible damage by the time they see a doctor.[21]

Coronary Heart Disease: The past two decades have seen much activity in the field of heart research. In some cases patients have been observed for as long as twenty years in order to try and isolate some of the causes of heart disease. At the same time, researchers have been studying, from every possible angle, the areas in which alcohol might be a contributory factory.

In 1959 the Tecumseh Health Study was begun at the University of Michigan.[22] This study was so named because it involved intensive physical examinations of virtually every inhabitant of Tecumseh, Michigan, a small town approximately fifty-five miles southwest of Detroit. This study covered a span of nearly ten years, with additional physical examinations in 1962-65 and 1967-69. Analysis of the data collected by Dr. B. M. Ullman and his associates uncovered some very interesting relationships between alcohol and coronary heart disease.

In this study, men were divided into three groups. *the abstainers; light drinkers,* those who drank four ounces or less per week; and *heavier drinkers,* those who drank more than four ounces per week. It should be noted that the "heavier drinkers" were not necessarily alcoholics. It was found that persons who never drink at all exhibited the same heart-attack rate as those that drank any other amount. There were no statistical differences in the three groups. At the same time, in the case of nondrinkers who had been drinkers at one time, the heart-attack rate was *three times* that of the rest of the group.

Naturally, this result caused a great deal of speculation. However, there is still no satisfactory explanation as to why the "reformed" drinkers should exhibit a higher heart-attack rate. There was no significant difference as regards other risk factors; blood pressure, smoking, cholesterol, and the like. It was noted that the majority of the reformed drinkers stopped drinking for what were generally cited to be "health reasons." The only possible explanation to come to light so far is that the reformed drinkers were unhealthier to begin with.

The obvious question is whether or not early drinking habits might have contributed to earlier poor health. The rate at which the reformed drinkers consumed alcohol seems to have been of no significance. Also, all of the reformed drinkers exhibited the same coronary rate regardless of the degree of the early drinking. Another interesting finding is that the coronary rate in the group of heavier drinkers was no higher than that seen in the group of abstainers. The conclusions drawn from this part of the study seem to indicate that there is no danger to the heart from moderate drinking.

There is a possible explanation for the fact that reformed drinkers seem more prone to heart attacks. Perhaps an organism accustomed to alcohol is weakened in some way when alcohol is denied it. This would mean that the actual act of stopping is the significant point.

This is hypothesis of course. There is no evidence that it is true.

There is also another possible explanation. It is well known that Americans tend to drink less as they age. It could be that a greater percentage of the former drinkers were older, a fact that in itself could be responsible for the increased heart-attack rate.

Generally, there are three main factors most often associated with coronary heart disease, blood pressure, blood cholesterol levels and cigarette smoking. Men over the age of forty who exhibit any or all of these factors are three times as prone to heart attack as other men. In order to clarify the connection between these factors and heart disease, the Tecumseh study examined the coronary disease rates of persons who exhibited these characteristics.

First, no consistent patterns emerged when high-risk and low-risk persons were compared with lifelong abstainers. Former drinkers still evidenced the highest rates of heart attack, although former drinkers with low cholesterol levels exhibited no evidence of heart disease whatsoever.

Second, although high-risk drinkers, as might be expected, exhibited disease rates consistently higher than low-risk groups, there is an apparent inconsistency. It seems that *regardless* of the risk factors involved, lifelong abstainers and former drinkers who also smoke have a higher disease rate than any other group. Among men with high cholesterol levels, the heavier drinkers are more prone to heart disease than are the lighter drinkers. Men with high blood pressure and high cholesterol exhibit a heart-attack rate four times higher than any other group.

Among heavy smokers there seem to be no differences in disease rates when comparisons are made between former smokers and lifelong abstainers. The significance of this cannot be explained, as the reasons

77

that the former drinkers stopped drinking were not always known.

Another study supports the findings of the Tecumseh study. This was the *Los Angeles study*.[23] It was conducted in much the same manner as the Tecumseh study and reached much the same conclusion; that alcohol is *not* a factor in coronary heart disease. There was a slightly lower rate of heart attack among the nondrinkers compared to the drinkers, but this difference is not considered statistically significant. There is also some evidence that persons who stop drinking are more likely to develop heart disease than those who do not. Otherwise, the two studies were consistent.

Summary: Coronary heart disease rates seem to be higher for those who abstain or who have stopped drinking than it is in those who have not stopped drinking. Alcohol appears to have no effect upon coronary heart disease, although many researchers feel that it *is* a definite factor in cardiomyopathy. Whether or not alcohol is actually protective is still open to conjecture.

In closing this section, some mention should be made of *beriberi heart disease*. This has long been associated with alcoholics, and although rare, it is still occasionally seen. It has been suggested that beriberi and alcohol cardiomyopathy might result from some of the same causes—malnutrition being the most important. Beriberi certainly is caused by nutritional deficiencies. Some researchers even suggest that it is more the result of vitamin deficiency than it is of alcohol.[17] Given our knowledge of the dietary habits of alcoholics, this would explain why beriberi has always been associated with alcohol consumption.

THE CENTRAL NERVOUS SYSTEM

Intoxication! This word is not generally understood. It is usually clear when a person is intoxicated, but we tend to discount it when the individual involved is a light or occasional drinker. This can sometimes be a mistake. For a substance to be *toxic*, it must be a poison. Therefore, the actual definition of intoxication indicates that one has been poisoned.

The most important aspect of alcohol is that it causes intoxication. Usually intoxication is not dangerous and at worst might cause a hangover. There have been instances, however, where a sudden intake of massive amounts of alcohol has resulted in death. How does this come about? Exactly what effect does alcohol have on the brain and the rest of the nervous system that causes us to see double, to slur our words, and to have difficulty with our coordination? The answers still elude us.

Most researchers agree that we become intoxicated when alcohol interacts with nerve cells membrane in the brain. The hypothesis upon which this is based is known as the *Hodgkin Theory of the Conduction of Nerve Impulses.*[24] In this theory, the nerve cell membrane is pictured as a sort of pump. This pump constantly moves sodium and potassium ions back and forth until a sudden change in the ability to move sodium is brought about by an increase in voltage. This is what is known as a nerve impulse. This explanation is greatly simplified, of course but it will give the reader some basic knowledge.

That intoxication occurs in the brain is a fact not generally appreciated. We tend to *feel* intoxication only in the manner in which it affects our bodies. It is the brain that is intoxicated nonetheless. Researchers theorize that alcohol has the ability to interfere with the transfer of ions across the nerve cell membrane, thus causing the effect of drunkenness.[25] It is also entirely possible that alcohol affects cerebral function by interrupting some other metabolic process in the cell, or by blocking nerve impulses. This could come about in this manner. Nerve impulses are transmitted in a process involving the release of certain chemicals into the spaces between the cells. These spaces are known as *synaptic clefts*. If alcohol can block the release of these fluids, nerve impulses will not flow properly.

At the moment, however, there is no clear explanation as to why alcohol affects us the way it does. Researchers generally tend to support the hypothesis based on the Hodgkin Theory, however.

THE BRAIN

Metabolism: The effects alcohol produces in the brain can be produced by other drugs as well. Although we do not know the mechanism, we do know the physical results. There is up to a 30 per cent decrease in the brain's ability to consume oxygen and a reduction in the brain's ability to utilize glucose. Due to these and other factors it seems likely that alcohol in intoxicating doses reduces the amount of energy that the brain needs. However, it does not reduce the brain's energy-producing capacity. All that is definitely known in this respect is that alcohol changes the content of certain substances that the brain uses, glucose in particular.

Nerve Cell Transmission: The effects of alcohol on the increase in voltage of nerve cells mentioned in conjunction with the Hodgkin Theory are not understood to any degree. Research has been contradictory. The theory is that alcohol affects the nerve impulses by interfering with the cell's ability to move ions back and forth. There is even evidence that alcohol decreases the ability of the nerve cells to remain in the resting state.

Synaptic Function: The synaptic cleft, located between the nerve cells, is a tiny area almost impossible to study. This is why there is no consensus as to the effects alcohol might exert on the synapses. Although there is a large amount of literature on the effects of alcohol on the chemicals that work in the synaptic clefts, there is still no firm evidence that these are directly affected by alcohol. This is because it has been impossible to study these neurotransmitter chemicals within the synaptic clefts themselves. They have so far been examined only outside the brain.

Ion Transport: Alcohol affects the active transport of ions into and out of most of the body's cells, including the brain cells. This transport is felt to be due to the action of an enzyme known as *sodium-potassium adenosine triphosphatase*. This enzyme is difficult to handle and study, but there is sufficient information available to indicate that it may be involved in the effect that alcohol has on the brain. More research will be needed before a direct connection can be shown, but the evidence to date indicates that researchers are moving in the right direction.

OTHER EFFECTS

Until recently, researchers were convinced that occasional drinking is not harmful, that the effects of intoxication are only temporary and pass away with no complications. Recent evidence, however, indicates that there is no safe limit as far as alcohol is concerned. It reveals that alcohol, in any quantity, damages and destroys both individual brain cells and groups of brain cells.[10]

Researchers have established a direct relationship between the quantity of alcohol we put into our bodies and its effect on certain portions of our brain. For example, the average man, after drinking two bottles of beer, will begin to feel relaxed and free of anxiety. This happens because the outer layer of the brain, the area concerned with worry and anxiety, is the first affected by alcohol. If blood alcohol levels rise higher, the motor areas are affected and there is difficulty in controlling the muscular systems. If still more alcohol enters the body, the midbrain is affected and the individual will become sleepy and perhaps enter a stupor. If more alcohol is taken, this stupor can become death.

As stated earlier, alcohol is known to have an effect on the brain's use of oxygen. This is supported by the fact that a sudden lack of oxygen, such as that experienced at high altitudes, produces the same sequence of symptoms as alcohol.

How the oxygen consumption of the brain is affected by alcohol has been a mystery until recently. Dr. M. H. Knisely, and his associates, have now come forward with a theory based on a peculiar phenomenon known as "blood sludging." Dr. Knisely has also been able to provide considerable scientific proof in support of this theory.

In the normal individual, blood moves through the body into ever smaller passages until it finally enters the capillaries. These are the smallest of all. It is through the walls of the capillaries that oxygen passes, nourishing the surrounding tissue. Since the blood transport system becomes smaller and smaller, it is necessary for the blood to be as liquid as possible for an adequate flow to be maintained.

For some unknown reason, certain diseases, such as malaria and typhoid fever, cause the red cells in the blood to clump together. These clumps can become quite large, and when they reach the capillaries they can totally clog the system. This prevents the blood's oxygen from reaching its goal. If this clumping, or sludging, is extensive, entire areas can become oxygen starved.

In the 1940's Dr. Knisely began observing blood sludging in the eyeballs of various subjects. The eyeball contains many capillaries that lie just underneath the transparent system of the lens. In order to observe certain blood-sludging conditions, Dr. Knisely had to find a substance that would allow him to control the clumping to a specific degree. He did—alcohol.

Dr. Knisely controlled the amounts of alcohol given

to animals and volunteers, determining the exact amount that would be present in the blood. He then observed the actual sludging conditions prevailing in the capillaries as a result of over fifty human diseases.

After it had been shown that alcohol could induce blood sludging, one question remained unanswered: were all of the capillaries in the body affected in the same manner? For the answer, Dr. Knisely examined rabbit tissue after the rabbits had been given alcohol. The rabbits exhibited blood-cell sludging in every organ examined.

How much alcohol does it take to affect the blood in this manner? This question was answered by studying the eye capillaries of both student volunteers and patients admitted to a private sanitarium over a seventeen-month period. It was found that as little as one glass of beer affects the eyeball capillaries to a noticeable degree. In the case of alcoholic patients, it was found that *any* increase in blood alcohol results in substantial sludging and decrease of blood-flow rate. In patients with high blood alcohol levels, it was found that large numbers of capillaries were completely blocked and that many had actually ruptured, causing a high incidence of hemorrhaging in the eye.

The conclusion reached was that high levels of alcohol almost certainly cause capillary blockage and rupture in the brain. This means that oxygen is not distributed to the brain in sufficient quantities and brain cells die. The brain cannot replace these cells and it seems certain that excessive alcohol intake will result in permanently impaired brain function.

Alcohol alters its own effect on the central nervous system. More and more is required to produce the same effect. This reduced sensitivity is what is known as *tolerance*. It is this tolerance that is thought to be one of the primary reasons alcohol becomes addictive.

There is a great deal of difference in the way that alcohol acts in the bodies of those who are heavy drinkers as opposed to those who are actually dependent on alcohol. The heavy drinker is usually lulled into the familiar state of relaxation and euphoria, while the person who is dependent on the drug is usually just the opposite. He or she may be nervous or anxious. Alcohol can bring on bouts of rebellion and aggressive behavior. The interesting point here, is that the alcoholic almost always suppresses the memory of these anxious, tense moments when sober. It seems to be only the pleasant aspects that are remembered.

There are other differences as well. The alcoholic can consume vast quantities of alcohol without showing the effects. Sometimes, a fifth or a quart of alcohol a day is consumed before the effects are noted. The alcoholic can also perform quite complicated tasks with no impairment of ability, even when there are amounts of alcohol in the blood which would totally incapacitate the occasional heavy drinker. The reason for this is not known. For many years it was thought that this difference in tolerance levels could be accounted for by a difference in metabolic rate. We now know, however, that alcoholics do not exhibit a significant difference in alcohol metabolism. Therefore, it has been concluded that the tolerance difference must be accounted for somewhere in the central nervous system.

Another dramatic difference in alcoholics is the effect that deprivation creates. The average drinker suffers no more than an occasional hangover, while the alcoholic exhibits all of the classic symptoms of drug withdrawal: hallucinations, confusion, convulsions, disorientation and extreme nervous disorder. This usually occurs from twenty-four to forty-eight hours after drinking has ceased.

Delirium tremens, the horror of all alcoholics, should not be confused with those withdrawal symptoms. This is a potentially lethal disorder complicated by severe autonomic and metabolic dysfunction.

The length of time an alcoholic will experience withdrawal symptoms will vary considerably from individual to individual. And what is interesting is that the amount of alcohol consumed and the length of time it took to consume it do not seem to be important factors in the severity of the withdrawal.

Sensation and Perception: The eyes do not seem to react adversely to alcohol. They are relatively insensitive to the drug. They react to very large amounts in much the same manner as they react to darkness. They become slightly more sensitive to dim light, but there is a decreased ability to distinguish between lights of different brightnesses. The eyes also require a longer adaptation time when moving from light areas into dark ones and vice versa. There is also a slightly impaired ability to distinguish certain colors, particularly red.

As far as the ear is concerned, the results are similar. Alcohol does not seem to affect the sensitivity of the ear to very faint sounds. It does affect discrimination between different sounds.

The senses of smell and taste are both profoundly affected by alcohol. They are dulled, even by relatively small amounts. The sense of touch is not noticeable affected, but the ability to withstand pain increases markedly as blood levels of alcohol rise. This accounts for the use of alcohol as an anesthetic in the early days of medicine.

There are also several studies which suggest that alcohol can alter the perception of time and space. Distances are underestimated and time appears to pass more slowly.[21]

The Emotions: There is no question that alcohol in moderate quantities produces a pleasant sensation. The high many people feel when drinking lowers their inhibitions and makes it easier to deal with others. This situation is, in part, due to the acceptance of intoxication by our culture. Our behavior is determined much more by social factors than it is upon whatever toxic effects alcohol might have on the brain.

85

Some researchers have shown a connection between alcohol and a reduced degree of fear. This can be a destructive tendency, as the individual concerned frequently takes needless risks that can be dangerous. Animal studies on cats have supported this contention. Cats which have been taught to fear electric shock lose this fear after ingesting alcohol.[21]

Reaction time is also affected by alcohol. This is essentially a function of the nervous system which controls how long the body takes to react to a stimulus. When blood alcohol levels are lower than .07 per cent, reaction time does not seem to be affected. Up to .10 per cent causes a slightly decreased reaction time. More than this affects reaction time to a marked degree.[21]

Studies on speed and accuracy have been conducted in relation to alcohol consumption. Speed is not adversely affected but accuracy is. In other words, an individual might complete an assigned task in record time and then find that the work is almost useless due to the number of errors made. At the same time, many subjects feel that their work actually improves when under the effects of alcohol and are amazed when the error rate is pointed out to them.[21]

Studies on the more esoteric phases of emotional response have also been conducted. In one study, humor was the object. It was found that alcohol does affect the perception of humor. In this study, a group of men were asked to rate a series of cartoons; some after drinking alcohol and some after drinking a placebo beverage. It was found that the cartoons were considered much funnier after alcohol ingestion, particularly those having to do with aggressive behavior. Nonsense humor was less appreciated.[21]

In studies during which *projective* tests have been administered, or tests which are designed to uncover hidden or concealed emotions, it was found that alcohol increases superficial, impulsive or disorganized responses. These responses have been connected with motor impairment and decreases in intellectual function.[21]

A test known as the *Thematic Apperception Test,* or TAT, has been widely used on alcoholics in order to assess alcohol's effect on fantasy. Administration of this test entails showing the subject a picture around which he or she is supposed to build some sort of story. In one such test, conducted in Finland, it was found that alcohol induces definite signs of uninhibited expression. These include both sexual and aggressive characteristics. In general, the stories created by those under the influence of alcohol were more unorganized and superficial than those created by sober subjects.[21]

In an American study, it was found that high alcohol-blood levels contribute to sexual and self-assertive states of being.[21]

Coordination: We know that alcohol has a debilitating effect on motor control. What is not generally known is that alcohol is selective; it affects some basic skills more than others.

Standing upright is markedly affected by alcohol, particularly when the eyes are covered and visual orientation is lost. The ability to concentrate is also impaired, especially when trying to keep track of two things at once.

Alcohol's effect on motor capabilities varies considerably from person to person, particularly when small amounts are involved. Too much alcohol will affect anyone, but some individuals seem to be able to overcome small amounts better than others. This ability seems to be related to character rather than to anything physical. Persons who are generally overachievers overcome the effects of alcohol more quickly than others.

Many studies have been designed to ascertain what amounts of alcohol need to be present before motor control is affected. One such study concerns a simulated driving test.[21] Various types of individuals were subdivided into two groups; the extroverts and the introverts. Generally speaking, extroverts made no alterations in speed during the test, and made more errors. The introverts varied their speed; some got faster, some got slower. They did not make as many errors, but there was more variation in the type of errors made. Also, alcohol had a more detrimental effect on those subjects who were poor drivers to begin with.

In another study, intellectual young men were confronted with problems in logic. In almost all cases, performance improved after small amounts of alcohol were ingested. After larger amounts, however, performance deteriorated considerably.[21]

Alcohol and Sex: Ever since Shakespeare said that alcohol, "provokes the desire but it takes away the performance," man has been aware of alcohol's effect on sexual performance. From casual observation, and in numerous cases from experience, many people conclude that alcohol has a beneficial effect upon sexual performance. This is not the case. Alcohol does loosen the control we have over our minds. It does allow a relaxed state in which we feel more amorous, more sexually interested. Our inhibitions vanish and we feel free to indulge in sex without the guilt that might normally be associated with it. All of these are emotional responses, however.

What about the physical response? Extensive studies on both animals and human beings prove conclusively that alcohol depresses sexual performance.[21] Studies show that alcoholics frequently lead markedly disturbed sex lives. And in subjects with a long history of alcoholism, there is a tendency toward premature senility, which includes impotency and actual degeneration of the sexual organs.

ALCOHOL AND THE BLOOD

The blood-supply system is so intimately involved with every part of the body that it is difficult to single

88

out particular effects that alcohol might have. One such case was the effect of red-cell sludging. However, there are many other blood difficulties that result from ingestion of alcohol. In the past, these difficulties have been attributed to a variety of other reasons; acute and chronic liver disease, and malnutrition and chronic infection, among others. Recent evidence, however, indicates that alcohol ingestion itself may severely affect the blood-supply system.[7] These symptoms, however, are apparently transitory and appear only after heavy alcohol consumption. The symptoms vanish, with or without treatment, as soon as alcohol intake is reduced.

Megaloblastic Anemia: This disease is common among alcoholics, particularly those who suffer from folic acid deficiency. For many years the disease was thought to be solely the result of inadequate food intake. Recent evidence indicates this is not just a dietary problem.[7]

Many researchers have studied the relationship between magaloblastic anemia and alcohol. These studies have been confused by the fact that some individuals develop this disease while others, who drink as heavily and eat as badly, do not. The most significant study in this area was conducted by Sullivan and Herbert in 1964.[26] Three malnourished patients with megaloblastic anemia caused by folic acid deficiency were fed a diet containing no folic acid. Vitamin supplements were provided, but these did not include folic acid or vitamin B_{12}. Folic acid was given separately in carefully controlled amounts of sufficient quantity to correct the megaloblastic anemia. Alcohol in the forms of whisky and wine were also given in order to gauge what effects they might have on the folic acid supplements. Whenever whisky was administered, the effects of the supplements were completely depressed. And the bone marrow, which had returned to normal, became anemic again whenever alcohol was consumed. Larger doses of folic acid were needed before the debilitating effects of the alcohol could be overcome.

The results of this study indicate that alcohol depresses the effects of small doses of folic acid, and that megaloblastic changes readily appear whenever alcohol is ingested by a subject whose vitamin stores are depressed and whose food intake is insufficient. Exactly why this happens is not clear. It does not seem to be associated with decreased folic acid absorption. This was proven by further experimentation. There is evidence that in the alcoholic who is drinking heavily and eating poorly, alcohol causes changes in the bone marrow and lining of the small intestine. This may indirectly contribute to the deficiency by causing an absorption problem. It is not the primary cause, however. What is the primary cause? No one knows.

GENES, CELLS AND ALCOHOL

There is considerable evidence that alcohol injures cell membranes.[9] This happens whether the diet is adequate or not. Liver cells are particularly vulnerable to this type of damage. However, in the case of all cell membranes, we know that a healthy structure is necessary for the transport of food materials. Alcohol disrupts this healthy membrane and incapacitates this transport function.

The metabolism of the cell membrane may also be affected by alcohol. But it is still difficult to pinpoint these effects, for they are extremely subtle. Their relationship to the membrane's structural changes after prolonged alcohol ingestion is not yet clearly understood.

There are many reasons for suspecting that the cellular membranes may be a specific target of alcohol poisoning. First, we know that alcohol affects the stability of most membrane structures. Second, this membrane is a definite factor in metabolic regulation, oxidation, synthesis, drug metabolism, nerve conductance and food transport. Third, membrane regeneration is very rapid and this makes it especially vulnerable to the action of drugs, particularly since the by-products of alcohol metabolism remain in membrane tissue and actually become part of the structure. This is why damage persists after alcohol has been taken away from the alcoholic.

There are also specific effects on membranes when alcoholic intake is high, although the mechanism by which these effects occur is still not known. We do know that certain tissue cells are more affected by alcohol than others, particularly liver cells. This is attributable, in part, to the fact that liver cells are more often exposed to high concentrations of alcohol than are other tissues.

The Genotrophic Origin: No discussion on the effect of alcohol on genes can be complete without some mention of the *genotrophic concept*. This is the theory that a taste or need for alcohol is genetic and is passed on from one generation to the next.[8]

No one suggests that the taste for alcohol itself is genetic, although that is certainly a possibility. The word genotrophic comes from two words: *geneto,* having to do with genes, or heredity, and *trophic,* having to do with feeding and nutrition. A genotrophic requirement has to do with an unusual nutritional need passed along genetically.

We know that genes carry the codes which make us what we are. Not many of us realize, however, that there are genes that work in relation to our nutritional needs. Genes are tiny particles, passed from parent to child, that dictate how we look and how our minds and bodies function. Genes are specialized, some are responsible for the production of certain enzymes our bodies need to stay healthy. These enzymes, in turn, are responsible for breaking down foods into elements small enough to be used. Sometimes, these genes be-

91

come blocked. When that happens, our enzyme-synthesizing ability also becomes blocked through genetic disease.

When this type of genetic disease appears, the individual reacts by needing a particular nutriment. When there is an oversupply of that nutriment, everything will very likely proceed normally. If there is not, and if the ingredient is easily obtainable from alcohol, alcoholism may result.

The first indication that there might be some validity in the genotrophic concept came about when research showed that alcoholic rats could be made to abstain by adding certain food elements to their diets. From these observations, and from observations taken in other studies, it would seem clear that some human beings might overindulge in alcohol due to a genotrophic need. And if the individual uses alcohol to meet this need the situation will be further complicated. Improper eating habits will inevitably result and deprive the individual the required minerals, proteins and vitamins needed to sustain health.

Another complication is the result of alcohol's ability to affect tissue membrane, which can impair the regulatory tissue in the hypothalamus. Since the hypothalamus controls the body's appetite, the loss of this control, coupled with poor nutrition, means that it would take an almost superhuman effort to abstain.

THE ENDOCRINES

The endocrine system contains the *thalamus* and *hypothalamus,* the *pancreas,* the *thyroid,* and the *adrenal glands,* among others. The effects of alcohol ingestion on the endocrines is clear. They are directly affected on alcohol and by the first product of alcohol oxidation, *acetaldehyde.* Both of these directly attack the hypothalamus, changing its normal activity patterns. Both also affect the cerebral cortex of the brain, creating strange patterns of physical activity and emotional behavior and disrupting the electron-transport system essential to the proper functioning of the central nervous system.[27]

Insulin, glucagon, growth hormone, cortisol and *epinephrine* are all hormones secreted by the endocrines. These are directly related to sugar metabolism, which is itself affected by alcohol. By its action on the hypothalamus, alcohol affects these substances even before they are secreted. It also affects them directly.

First, it stimulates their flow. Second, it causes what is known as oxidation-reduction. This reduces hormones to a simpler, less active form. Third, it affects the blood sugar level.

Insulin, for example, decreases blood sugar by increasing oxidation and by speeding the change from blood sugar to glycogen, which is sugar in its stored form. Cortisol, on the other hand, increases blood sugar by raising production levels and interfering with its oxidation. The other endocrine substances increase blood sugar by mobilizing available supplies of glycogen and converting them back into free sugar.[27] So, while insulin is working to decrease blood sugar, the other hormones, produced by the artificial stimulation of alcohol, are trying to increase it. The effects should be obvious.

There are also indirect effects. Take insulin again. Its secretion is primarily dependent on blood-sugar levels, not on alcohol ingestion. However, as alcohol is directly responsible for blood-sugar changes due to its action on other hormones, it also indirectly affects insulin.

Researchers have shown that an adequate supply of blood sugar is protection against insulin rise when alcohol is present. In studies where both alcohol and sugar have been given, however, blood sugar has risen higher than it would have with sugar alone.[27]

In 1972 researchers conducted a study in which subjects were asked to fast for three days. Naturally, their blood-sugar levels went down, and consequently their insulin levels. Alcohol was then administered. Both blood-sugar and insulin levels continued to fall.[28]

Alcohol appears to have considerable effect on the hormone-secreting system and its products. How this occurs is not yet clear. More studies need to be made.

We have seen how alcohol affects the heart, the endocrines, the cells, the genes and the central nervous system. In the next chapter, we will examine specific alcohol-related illnesses.

REFERENCES AND ADDITIONAL READING FOR CHAPTER FIVE

1. Marks, V., Chakraborty, J., "The Clinical Endocrinology of Alcoholism," *The Journal on Alcoholism*, Vol. 8, No. 3, Autumn, 1973.
2. Murdock, H. R., Jr., "Thyroidal Effect of Alcohol," *Quarterly Journal on the Study of Alcoholism*, Vol. 28, No. 3, September, 1967.
3. Baum, R., Iber, F. L., "Alcohol, the Pancreas, Pancreatic Inflammation, and Pancreatic Insufficiency," *American Journal on Clinical Nutrition*, Vol. 26, No. 3, March, 1973.
4. Aull, J. C., *et al.*, "Rate of Metabolism of Ethanol in the Rat," *American Journal of Physiology*, 186, 380, 1956.
5. Gradiner, R. J., Stewart, H. B., "Blood Alcohol and Glucose Changes after Ingestion of Ale, Wine and Spirit," *Quarterly Journal on the Study of Alcoholism*, Vol. 29, No. 2, June, 1968.
6. Rutter, L. F., "A Study of Lactate and Pyruvate Levels in Blood and Urine Samples from Abstinent Alcoholics and Their Biochemical Significance," *Journal on Alcoholism*, Vol. 6, No. 2, Summer, 1971.
7. Lindenbaum, J., "Hematologic Effects of Alcohol," *Biology of Alcoholism*, Vol. 3.
8. Williams, R. J., *Alcoholism: The Nutritional Approach*, University of Texas Press, Austin, 1972.
9. French, S. W., "Acute and Chronic Toxicity of Alcohol," *Biology of Alcoholism*, Vol. 1, Chapter 14.
10. Maisel, A. Q., "Alcohol and Your Brain," *Reader's Digest*, June, 1970.
11. Sullivan, J. F., *et al.*, "Myocardiopathy of Beer Drinkers: Subsequent Course," *Annual on Internal Medicine*, Omaha, 1968.

12. Alexander, C. S., "Idiopathic Heart Disease. II. Electron Microscopic Examination of Miocardial Biopsy Specimens in Alcoholic Heart Disease," *American Journal of Medicine*, 41: 229, 1966.

13. Ammon, H. P. T., Estler, C. J., "Influence of Acute and Chronic Administration of Alcohol on Carbohydrate Breakdown and Energy Metabolism in the Liver," *Nature*, 216: 158, 1969.

14. Ashworth, C. T., *et al.*, "Cellular Aspects of Ethanol-Induced Fatty Liver: A Correlated Ultrastructural and Chemical Study," *Journal on Lipid Research*, 6:258, 1965.

15. Augustine, J. R., "Laboratory Studies in Acute Alcoholics," *Canadian Medical Association Journal*, 96: 1367, 1967.

16. Burch, G. E., Walsh, J. J., "Cardiac Insufficiency in Chronic Alcoholism," *American Journal on Cardiology*, 6:864, 1960.

17. Alexander, C. S., "Idiopathic Heart Disease. 1. Analysis of 100 Cases with Special Reference to Chronic Alcoholism," *American Journal of Medicine*, 41:213, 1966.

18. Wilens, S. L., "Relationship of Chronic Alcoholism to Atherosclerosis," *Journal of the American Medical Association*, 135:1136-39, 1947.

19. Kannel, W. B., Gordin, T., (eds.), "The Framingham Study: An Epidemiological Investigation of Cardiovascular Disease," *Section 26*, Washington, D.C., 1971.

20. Burch, G. E., DePasquale, N. P., "Alcoholic Cardiomyopathy," *Cardiologia*, 52:48-56, 1968.

21. U. S. Department of Health, Education and Welfare, *First Special Report to the U. S. Congress on Alcohol and Health for the Secretary of Health, Education and Welfare*, Washington, D.C., 1971.

22. Ullman, B. M., *et al.*, "Alcoholic Consumption and Coronary Heart Disease," *Final Report to the National Institute on Alcohol Abuse and Alcoholism*, 1974.

23. Chapman, J. M., *et al.*, "A Study of the Relationship Between Alcohol Consumption and Heart Disease," *Final Report to the National Institute on Alcohol Abuse and Alcoholism*, 1974.

24. Hodgkin, A. L., "Ionic Movements and Electrical Activity in Giant Nerve Fibers," *Procedures of* . . . . *Sociology*, London Biologists, 1958.

25. Pauling, L. A., "A Molecular Theory of General Anesthesia," *Science*, 134:15-21, 1961.

26. Sullivan, J. F., *et al.*, "Folic Acid Metabolism in Alcoholics," *American Journal on Clinical Nutrition*, 1964.

27. Axelrod, D. R., "Metabolic and Endocrine Aberrations in Alcoholism," *Biology of Alcoholism*, 1973.

28. Hagdade, J. D., *et al.*, "Counterregulation of Basal Insulin Secretion During Alcohol Hypoglycemia in Diabetic and Normal Subjects," *Diabetes*, 21:65, 1972.

CHAPTER SIX

ALCOHOL: Related Illnesses and Disease

CANCER

For many years, researchers have observed a definite association between heavy drinking and cancer of the mouth, pharynx, larynx, esophagus and liver. This has led to a series of studies designed to trace the possible connection between alcohol and these cancers. To date, no attempts to produce cancer in test animals by administering large amounts of alcohol have been successful. There is considerable evidence to suggest, however, that the risks of contracting cancer are increased by prolonged exposure to alcohol.

As far back as 1910 a link between alcohol and cancer was suggested. Lamu, a French researcher, was able to draw a connection between cancer of the esophagus and the drinking of absinthe, an alcoholic beverage containing 75 per cent alcohol and flavored with wormwood,[23] a carcinogen now banned. No further substantial work in this area took place until almost 1950 when the relationship between cigarette smoking and cancer was first widely recognized. This was the beginning of much activity designed to establish a connection between various forms of cancer and personal habits. Naturally, drinking came under study.

Studies on alcoholics are always complicated by the difficulty in obtaining adequate case histories. Normal dietary patterns are therefore difficult to establish. It is also difficult to determine how much alcohol the subject might have ingested. The difficulty is even further compounded by the fact that alcoholics also tend to be heavy smokers. This makes it extremely difficult to determine which factor—drinking or smoking—is most important in cancer-related problems. It is almost impossible to study the two separately.

The process by which alcohol might cause cancer is unknown, but there have been a number of suggestions. Among these are the effects of prolonged and repeated physical contact with alcohol, especially if alcohol is normally ingested in strong, spirit solutions. Another suggestion concerns the possible synergistic factor in the combination of alcohol and tobacco. Still another theory is that alcohol might trigger some other mechanism, a virus perhaps, turning it into a carcinogen. And there are all the indirect contributions of alcohol—malnutrition, anemia and bad hygiene. Any of these could be a factor in cancer.

The Mouth, Pharynx and Larynx: These cancer sites are part of an area in which cancer is frequently seen in male alcoholics.[24] This suggests some sort of connection between such cancers and heavy drinking. It has been established that both smoking and drinking contribute to the formation of these diseases, and that in concert their effects are even more pronounced. One study has found that tobacco and alcohol together augment the carcinogenic effects of a chemical called *7-14-dimethylbenzanthracene*.[25]

Cancer of the mouth is common among heavy drinkers. Indeed, tobacco is named as the chief cause of this type of cancer throughout the world. When alcohol is added, the risk factor is increased proportionately.

In one group of alcoholics studied, it was discovered that 93 per cent of the men and 91 per cent of the women were heavy smokers. This is a much higher percentage than that exhibited by the rest of the population.[26] Another study found a close relationship between drinking and smoking ratios and cancers of different parts of the mouth and throat.[6] Those who drink more than they smoke exhibit a higher incidence of cancer of the floor of the mouth. Those who smoke more than they drink evidence more cancer of the roof of the mouth, and of the other areas where inhalation brings tobacco smoke into contact with tissue. Another outcome of this study was a link connecting different types of alcohol with cancer. It was found that alcoholics who drink distilled spirits are more susceptible to cancer of the ingestion tract.

In the late 1950's, in a series of studies conducted by E. L. Wynder,[27] it was discovered that patients with oral or laryngeal cancers tend to be heavy drinkers. Dr. Wynder concluded that as the amount of ingested alcohol increases, the risks of cancer of the mouth, larynx and esophagus also increase—as much at ten times! He even suggested that smoking might initiate cancer and alcohol contribute to it.

In 1963 Dr. Keller and his associates found there was a "strongly positive association between drinking more than 1.6 oz. of absolute alcohol per day plus smoking forty or more cigarettes per day and cancer of the mouth and pharynx."[28] In other studies, lung cancer was found to be associated with tobacco but not with alcohol. Similarly, no connection was found between alcohol and stomach cancer or cancer of the mouth.

In 1962 a massive French study concerned the drinking habits of 3,937 cancer patients.[29] Another group was also involved; 1,807 patients who were scrutinized in order to trace any possible link between their cancers and alcohol and tobacco. It was determined that patients with cancer of the mouth, hypopharynx, larynx and esophagus were much heavier drinkers than the corresponding members of a control group—even after the figures were adjusted for tobacco use. Excessive alcohol intake also seemed particularly evident in those suffering from cancer of esophagus and other parts of the aerodigestive tract.

A group of researchers in Canada report that the cancer rate of the upper aerodigestive tract is five times higher among Toronto's alcoholics than among the general population.

In an American study involving almost two thousand subjects, researchers found that alcoholics exhibit almost four times the normal incidence of cancer of the mouth, pharynx, larynx, esophagus and lungs.[30] It should be mentioned that smoking was not taken into account in either of those studies. This factor could be the reason for the mention of lung cancer, a disease not usually associated with alcohol consumption.

The Pancreas: The pancreas is primarily responsible for excreting and maintaining the body's supply of insulin, an important factor in maintaining adequate levels of blood sugar.

Other Cancer Sites: There has been a certain amount of investigation into cancer of the prostate gland and its possible connection to alcohol. No one has been able to find a direct connection, however, and more research is being conducted.

It was previously mentioned that some research has shown no connection between cancer of the stomach and alcohol. This is true, especially in the light of the fact that cancer of the stomach is becoming rarer and consumption of alcohol is increasing. One study, however, did reveal that cancer of the upper portion of the stomach, the so-called *cardiac-stomach,* seems to be present in a high proportion of alcoholics. More men were involved as well, giving a certain amount of support to the existence of a connection between alcohol and this type of cancer.[33] As of this moment there is little evidence in this area that might be called conclusive. It is generally felt that other factors are probably responsible for the high level of stomach cancer in alcoholics.

How Does Alcohol Affect Cancer?: As a result of some of these studies, additional research has been undertaken to try and find the mechanism by which alcohol become a cancer factor. At the moment, the appearance of cancer is considered attributable to a combination of factors—alcohol being only one.

It is relatively definite that alcohol and smoking together can be extremely dangerous. It might be synergistic—the effects of the two factors might be greater than their sum. In other words, the risk of developing cancer from either smoking or drinking alone is quite high, but the risk of getting cancer when both factors are present is much higher.

Strong alcohol solutions are directly irritating to mucous membrane tissue. This in itself might be a factor in cancer. At the same time it might cause the affected tissue to become more sensitive to other carcinogens. Alcohol might also serve as a transport medium for trace elements that might be carcinogenic.

Malnutrition could also be a contributing factor. It is possible that alcoholic malnutrition could weaken the entire system, making it an easy target for carcinogenic substances. Deficiencies of protein, iron, vitamins and minerals have been associated with other types of cancer.

Lastly, alcoholic liver damage may lead to an altered metabolism of certain carcinogenic substances, enhancing their cancer-causing effects.

Summary: Studies have indicated that alcohol is a factor in cancer, especially among those who smoke heavily. Cancers of the mouth, larynx, pharynx and esophagus appear again and again in those who combine these two substances in excessive quantities. Cancer of the esophagus seems to be most prevalent among those who take hard spirits. There also seems to be a connection between alcohol and cancer of the pancreas.

THE ENCEPHALOPATHIES

Alcohol abuse is clearly a factor in weakening the system and making it vulnerable to attack by pathological agents. In others it is direct. Excessive alcohol is associated with nutritional deficiencies of such vital substances as folic acid, niacin, and thiamin, which may themselves be responsible for any number of other diseases.

Among the most serious of these are the encephalopathies. These include *niacin-deficiency encephalopathy, Korsakoff's Psychosis, Wernicke's Syndrome,* and *Marchiafava's Disease.*[35]

Niacin-deficiency Encephalopathy: This disease is also known as *Jolliffe's encephalopathy,* and is characterized by clouding of the consciousness, rigid arms and legs, and sucking and grasping reflexes. It is fatal if treatment is delayed, but it responds well to massive doses of niacin and other B-complex vitamins. It is frequently found among advanced alcoholics.

Korsakoff's Psychosis: This is primarily a mental disorder. It is characterized by disorientation, memory failure, and an odd tendency to pretend that imagined occurences have actually taken place. It sometimes follows on the symptoms of other encephalopathic diseases and is therefore suspected to be partially the result of a thiamin deficiency. If sufferers of this disease do not respond to treatment quickly it can become a prolonged disability, requiring lengthy hospitalization.

Wernicke's Syndrome: This disease is associated with an acute, severe deficiency of vitamin B_1. It is characterized by a clouding of the consciousness and paralysis of the eye nerves. These conditions respond well to thiamin treatment.

Marchiafava's Disease: This disease is not common. It is a degeneration of the *corpus callosum* area of the brain, and it causes severe mental dysfunction. It is complicated to diagnose as its symptoms are never specific. Usually, correct diagnosis is not made until the patient is dead.

THE GASTROINTESTINAL TRACT

The interaction between the gastrointestinal system and alcohol has not been as heavily studied as have other areas of the body. Still there is sufficient indication that large quantities of alcohol are definitely a factor in diseases of this area.

It has long been assumed that alcohol affects the system after it is absorbed. Recently, however, evidence has accumulated that suggests that very strong spirits might be a more direct problem; might directly irritate the gastrointestinal tissues with which they come in contact.

The Stomach: Whenever alcohol enters the mouth, acid is secreted in the stomach. In addition, alcohol delays the emptying time of the stomach. These two factors, in combination, might cause a hyperacidic condition, which in time could promote stomach disorder.

Alcohol also affects the passage of hydrogen ions out of the stomach and the passage of sodium and potassium ions into it. This ability to alter the electrical properties of the stomach is direct evidence that alcohol can do damage in that area.[34]

Gastrititis and *achlorhydria* are quite common in alcoholics, as are gastric ulcers. More than half of the patients who suffer from massive hemorrhage in the upper gastric area have been found to have ingested alcohol, aspirin, or both, shortly before the commencement of bleeding.[12]

The Small Intestine: Diseases of this area are not often a complication in alcoholism, but this does not mean that they are not a problem when they do occur. Neither is it intended to suggest that alcohol is not a factor in diseases of the small intestine. Some researchers maintain that alcohol impairs absorption in the small intestine, *even when nutrition is adequate.*[12]

Alcoholics frequently suffer decreased absorption of folic acid, fat, and vitamin B_{12}. Also, in various animal experiments it has been seen that large doses of alcohol interfere with the body's ability to pass amino acids through the intestinal walls. Why this happens is not known. But these problems tend to be reversible with treatment.[20]

The Pancreas: Excessive alcohol intake is associated with *pancreatitis* and *pancreatic insufficiency.* Alcoholic patients almost always evidence a loss of the ability of the pancreas to react to stimulation. Fortunately, this is reversible.

Pancreatitis may directly result from alcohol damage or may be attributable to a combination of alcohol and a muscular spasm in what is known as the *sphincter of Oddi.* This spasm partially closes off the pancreatic duct and increases pressure in that area at the same time that alcohol increases the secretion of gastric acid and causes additional secretion from the pancreas. This worsens the pressure in the duct and favors the development of pancreatitis.

THE MUSCULAR SYSTEM

For at least a hundred and fifty years medical researchers have noticed muscular weakness in alcoholics. It was not until 1957, however, that a defined syndrome of muscle disease was recognized in the United

States. This syndrome is frequently a complication of alcoholism.

There are three forms of this disease: *subclinical myopathy, acute alcoholic myopathy*, and *chronic alcoholic myopathy*.[8]

Subclinical Myopathy: This disease is difficult to recognize as there is sometimes a total lack of symptoms. This no-symptoms condition, however, can cause an increase of certain elements in the blood; notably an enzyme known as *creatine phosphokinase* (CPK). Most patients committed to hospitals after prolonged drinking sprees exhibit a raised level of CPK. In other cases, however, this enzyme may be at normal levels. Also, sufferers of subclinical myopathy frequently exhibit a rise in blood levels of lactic acid.

Acute Alcoholic Myopathy: This disease appears in several forms. In some patients it is characterized by sudden muscular cramps that vary in frequency and are often short lived. Usually, these occur in the muscles of the arms and legs, but there have also been reports of spasms in the abdominal wall.

A dramatic form of this disease is evidenced by the appearance of muscle pigment in the urine. This is called *myoglobinuria*. It usually appears after very heavy drinking and causes severe pain and swelling in the muscles as well as significant weakness. This type of alcoholic myopathy is found in chronic alcoholism and is generally associated with severe liver disease. Recovery is possible if the patient abstains from alcohol and if acute kidney failure has not already taken place.

As the body repairs itself, the pain and swelling will gradually disappear. This does not necessarily mean that the disease is gone. It is possible to move into *chronic alcoholic myopathy* without any further signs of the acute form being present.

Chronic Alcoholic Myopathy: This form of the disease can come almost unexpectedly. It is an insidious disease appearing after prolonged alcohol

107

ingestion or after sudden outbreaks of its acute form. It is characterized by weakness and muscle atrophy, which may appear anywhere in the body but is most often associated with the legs.

Both acute and chronic alcoholic myopathy are associated with changes in the muscle tissue. While studying these changes through a microscope, it has been observed that focal atrophy of individual muscle cells is quite common in the subclinical form of the disease.

The mechanism that triggers this disease is still unknown. Nutritional deficiency has been suggested, as has direct alcohol action on the muscles. It is clear, however, that alcohol is the primary factor in the development of this disease.

DISEASES OF THE ENDOCRINES

We have seen that the endocrine system is essential to the body's health and well being. It is an extremely sensitive apparatus that controls the body's internal environment. So, when alcohol is consumed often enough to disturb the body's internal balance, it is quite clear that the endocrine system must react in one way or another. It must adapt itself to another set of governing rules.

By far the greatest amount of research on the endocrines and alcohol concerns what is known as the *hypothalamic-pituitary-adrenal* axis (HPA axis). As early as 1948 it was suggested that some sort of deficiency in this area might predispose some individuals toward alcoholism. There was at least some superficial evidence in support of this contention. It seems that Addison's disease, which is an adrenal-cortical insufficiency, exhibits symptoms similar to those seen in delirium tremens. It was concluded therefore, that alcoholism must be related to the endocrine glands, and many unsupported papers were written proclaiming the effectiveness of adrenal-cortical extracts in combating the later stages of alcoholism. As time passed, however, such claims were scrutinized more closely, and the practice of treating alcoholics with hormones was questioned.

How does alcohol act on the HPA axis? Research indicates that alcohol stimulates the pituitary into releasing the adrenocorticotropic hormone. This is the substance that triggers the adrenal cortex.[36]

In searching for deficiencies in the HPA axis, many defects have been found and described. Nothing conclusive has come from this search, however, as the studies involved have resulted in inconsistencies. Also, comparisons between the HPA axis of alcoholics and control persons have been complicated by a number of variables. These include nutritional problems and other illnesses that might be present, the use of illicit and prescription drugs, stress, and the emotional state of the subject. There is still no certain evidence that the HPA axis plays any part in predisposing the individual toward alcoholism. Damage found in that area, therefore, is usually attributed to the direct action of alcohol itself.

There is evidence that alcohol might affect another type of adrenal hormone, *aldosterone*. This substance causes retention of potassium, sodium and chloride in the tissues. Other affected harmones are the *catecholamines,* of which adrenalin is one, and *dopamine*. Animal and clinical studies have found that alcohol induces excessive secretion of these substances. It is also known to be a factor in upsetting the metabolism of the catecholamines.

Alcohol exerts a powerful effect on urinary excretion. This has long been observed by researchers and laymen alike, and experiments have confirmed the observation. This is attributable to alcohol's effect on the body's water balance. It inhibits the antidiuretic hormone secreted by the posterior pituitary. Any irregularity in this substance upsets water balance and causes the kidneys to excrete excessive amounts. This partially explains the dehydration that occurs after heavy drinking.

Alcohol also inhibits the secretion of a hormone known as *oxytocin*. This is necessary in stimulating contraction of the uterus. It is also a secretion of the posterior pituitary gland.

The *Silvestrini-Corda* syndrome is suffered by males. It is a clinical triad, having to do with a combination of three symptoms: *alcoholic liver cirrhosis, atrophy of the male sex glands,* and *enlargement of the breast.* At first, it would appear that this might be connected with increased estrogen levels. Several researchers, however, have discovered that estrogen levels in men suffering from alcoholic cirrhosis are generally within normal ranges. The mechanism of this condition is still unknown.

Alcoholic hypoglycemia, or low blood sugar, is another disease of the endocrines. It is caused by alcohol's interference with the pancreas and its secretion of insulin.[7]

In 1972 F. G. Greer conducted a study in which information from various alcoholics and their families was examined. Dr. Greer found that all recovered alcoholics, together with some of their relatives, were hypoglycemic. This tended to be chronic and was apparently the result of a dysfunction in the *hypo-adrenocortical* system.

Also (as hypo-adrenocorticalism is a stress disease, it can conceivably be passed on to other members of the family. Taking early case histories and the fact that this disease is so often seen in the families of alcoholics as a basis, Dr. Greer concluded that adrenocortical insufficiency might in some way induce alcohol add addiction. If this is true then the existance of this disease among the children of alcoholics supports the contention that alcoholism is an hereditary disease.

Hypo-adrenocorticalism is a complicated disease. When no alcohol is present, or when the alcoholic has become an abstainer, it can be mistaken for neurosis, manic depression, schizophrenia or general depression. Persons with this disease are usually meticulous and have a perfectionist view toward work. They frequently evidence high I.Q.'s and are frequently either over or under achievers. They are also usually heavy smokers.

ALCOHOL AND PREGNANCY

Evidence suggests that women who drink heavily should not do so while pregnant. A study conducted in 1972 at the University of Washington found that alcoholic women are likely to produce children with serious birth defects.[16]

On group of English researchers recently described eight cases where alcoholic mothers gave birth to deformed children.[17] All of the concerned babies had lower-than-normal intelligence. They all weighed less and were shorter than average. Most were unable to respond well to simple motor-skill tests and were afflicted with certain physical abnormalities, such as heart murmurs, unformed limbs and facial characteristics. The growth patterns of all of the children were permanently retarded.

The only connection between the mothers of these children was that they were all alcoholics and had all been drinking heavily during pregnancy. They were of mixed racial origin and came from different economic groups. None exhibited genetic damage.

It is not clear how these deformities are caused by alcohol, but results of this study, and others, have led researchers to conclude that as many as 20 per cent of all alcoholic mothers will give birth to deformed children.

Not only is the mother suspect in this instance, but recent animal studies have indicated that the fathers might also contribute to this problem through alcohol-damaged sperm. Dr. F. M. Badr and his wife, Ragaa S.

Badr have conducted experiments that support the contention that heavy drinking in fathers may cause spontaneous abortion and birth defects.[37]

The Badr's experiment was conducted using male mice. In the first experiment they fed eight male mice with alcohol for three days. The mice received the equivalent of about four drinks a day. Each of these mice were then mated once a week for six weeks. The offspring were then examined.

The litters were normal except for that litter which was conceived fourteen days after alcohol ingestion had stopped. This suggests that sperm is susceptible to alcohol at particular stages of the ripening process.

The second phase of the experiment attempted to pinpoint the effects of male drinking. Nineteen male mice were made alcoholic. They were then mated with different females every four days. The litter sizes remained the same for both alcoholic males and control males. However, there was a marked increase in the number of dead embryos found in the mates of the drinking mice, especially those who had conceived from nine to thirteen days after drinking had ceased. The results again confirmed the hypothesis that alcohol can lead to spontaneous abortion by damaging sperm at a certain stage of its development.

As far as human subjects are concerned, there have been no carefully controlled studies designed to link drinking in men with birth defects. One preliminary study has been conducted by Dr. Badr and several researchers working at St. Vincent's Hospital in Worcester, Massachusetts.[38] Fifty-two fathers who are heavy drinkers were examined. Each had consumed at least four drinks a night for at least six weeks prior to conception. A higher-than-normal level of spontaneous abortion and birth defects were noted among the offspring. This was a pilot study, however, and cannot be considered conclusive. Much more work must take place in this field before a link between male alcoholism and birth defects can be proved.

SLEEP AND ALCOHOL

The study of sleep is relatively new. This is surprising considering that it is one of our most basic biological processes. But the reason sleep was ignored for so long is simple—for years it seemed that sleep was a passive state where very little, if anything, actually happened. We now know that this is not true. Sleep is a complex phenomenon. It is a constantly changing, cyclical pattern of mind states that is simply different from waking states.

The study of an individual's sleep patterns begins immediately before the period of drowsiness. This may seem odd, but it is a convenience based on the idea that the brain must be in a state of activity before it can change. The alpha state is associated with being awake. This state is evidenced by electrical brain rhythms of from eight to twelve cycles per second. With the onset of drowsiness the alpha state alternately appears and disappears, gradually giving way to the theta state. This is characterized by rhythms of from four to six cycles per second. This is known as stage-one sleep.

State one continues for several minutes. During this period the brain rhythms decrease in number and get stronger until the mind slips into stage two. This is the sigma state, which is characterized by rhythms of twelve to fifteen cycles per second. Some researchers consider this second state the true onset of sleep. It is at this point that K-complexes appear. These are very brief and are superimposed on the normal sigma electrical patterns. They can be stimulated by any sensual input and are thought to be signs of sexual arousal.

After several minutes of stage-two sleep, stage three appears. This is characterized by high voltage delta

113

waves with a frequency of one to four cycles per second. In stage three, these delta waves appear at seemingly random intervals until, gradually, they increase in duration and stage four appears. In stage four the delta waves are also prominent.

Normally, the individual moves rapidly through all four sleep stages, remaining in stage four for approximately half an hour. After that, the process is reversed and moves back through stages three, two, and finally one. It is during this last stage one period that rapid eye movements, or REM, occur. It is during this stage that most dreaming takes place.

During a normal night's sleep, these cyclical patterns repeat themselves every ninety to one hundred minutes. As the repeats take place, the time spent in stage four is shortened and the time spent in stage one (REM sleep) is lengthened. REM sleep accounts for about 20 per cent of the total night's sleep.[14]

The Effects of Alcohol on the Sleep Cycle: In experiments on the effects of alcohol on sleep patterns, the findings have been remarkably consistent.

In the first study, conducted in 1933, the alcoholic equivalent of one quart of light wine was administered to four young adults forty-five minutes before bedtime. Body movements and rectal temperatures were recorded throughout the night. It was found that alcohol caused a marked reduction in both movement and body temperature during the first half of the night, and an increase in both during the second half. This was the first indication that sleep might be more than a passive state.[14]

In 1963 researchers examined the effects of alcohol on REM sleep, one the most important manifestations of normal mental activity during sleep.[14] The subjects were studied for five nights. On two nights they received either alcohol or caffeine. On the other three nights they drank only orange juice. The alcohol caused a significant decrease in the amount of REM sleep experienced by the seven volunteers, while the caffeine had no effect whatsoever.

In 1966 and '67 Yules and his associates conducted two series of experiments concerned with the effects of repeated doses of alcohol on the sleep of young men. In the first phase the subjects were studied for a total of thirteen nights. After first determining the normal sleeping patterns of the subjects, the effects of large amounts of alcohol were studied. The last four nights were devoted to the observation of the recovery patterns.

On the first alcoholic night, REM sleep decreased. On the next, however, it increased. This continued for several nights until the amounts of REM sleep exceeded that seen during the initial observation period. This increased pattern continued through part of the recovery period as well. By the fourth night, however, normal patterns had completely returned.

The initial decreases in REM sleep took place during the first half of the night, while the succeeding increases were confined to the second half of the night. Since it was only the length of REM sleep that was affected rather than the number of REM cycles, it was concluded that alcohol alters the mechanism that controls sleep-stage duration and does not affect the number of individual cycles.[14]

The second stage of the experiment was conducted along the same lines, and the researchers concluded that "it is the immediate and perhaps direct effect of alcohol itself on the nervous system centers that initiates the changes in sleep stages noted on alcohol nights."

Disturbed Sleep Patterns in Alcoholic Subjects: Extreme sleep disturbances in alcoholics have been noted for many years. It wasn't until 1959, however, that a systematic study of this problem was undertaken. Gross and Goodenough wrote in 1968:

115

In reconstructing the clinical histories of our patients, there is often an initial insomnia associated with the onset of the drinking episode. In fact, some of the patients describe this as the apparent precipitating factor in that only after consuming large quantities of alcohol can they sleep. This is usually followed by a variable period of heavy drinking which at first is not manifestly associated with sleep disturbances other than the need for alcohol in order to sleep.... Gradually, nightmares develop. At first they do not interrupt sleep but with time they cause increasing disturbance and disruption... after a transitional phase, which many report, in which the patient is uncertain as to whether he is asleep and having a nightmare, or awake and hallucinating, the patient enters a predominantly sleepless state associated with hallucinations.

Recent sleep research has shown that sleep deprivations, particularly of REM sleep, results in impairment of brain function, a lowering of the metabolic rate, illusions and hallucinations, and the appearance of psychotic symptoms.

Summary: In spite of the enormous amount of activity in this area during the past few years, we still do not know enough about the effects of alcohol consumption on sleep. However, we do know that even moderate doses of alcohol, single or repeated, cause an early onset of sleep, a slight increase in the heart and lung rate, and an inhibition of the REM stage.[14]

In a drinking bout, total sleeplessness is the final result. General sleep research has shown that total sleeplessness, or even an inhibition of the REM stages, produce negative results in the functioning of the brain and the metabolism, and also contribute to hallucinations and psychotic behavior. Alcohol can only make matters worse!

ALCOHOL AND NERVE DISORDERS

The nervous system is closely connected with alcohol's effects on the body. Earlier we saw how alcohol affects this system and how it is considered to be damaging to the health of the brain. In this section we will examine specific alcohol-related nervous system disorders.

Alcohol has many effects on the nervous system. The most common are inebriation and elevated blood-alcohol levels. These are followed by symptoms of alcoholic withdrawal: delusions, delirium tremens, hallucinations, etc. In addition, there are diseases and disorders associated with the nutritional deficiencies so often seen in the heavy, compulsive drinker. Generally speaking, the symptoms of inebriation and alcoholic withdrawal are reversible. They will respond well to treatment and abstinence. Unfortunately, the nutritional diseases are often not reversible. They frequently cause serious damage to the central nervous system that can never be repaired.

Considering that the symptoms of alcoholism have been so heavily documented, it is surprising that more is not known about the effects of prolonged exposure of the nervous system to alcohol. For instance, we still have no idea how alcohol breaks down in the body. We also have no idea as to how impurities in alcoholic beverages might affect the system. What we do know is that alcohol is responsible for the breakdown of dietary habits that leads to neurological disease.

As we have seen, when an alcoholic is drinking, his dietary habits change. There is a decrease in appetite caused by alcohol's contribution of calories. At the same time, the gastrointestinal system reacts in various ways; vitamin absorption may decrease, transport of other substances across the intestinal lining may be impaired; tissue storage and utilization and conversion to biologically active forms may be curtailed; all these

117

effects at a time when the alcoholic can least afford them.

Hypovitaminosis, or acute lack of vitamins, especially those found in the B-complex vitamins, appears to be a primary factor in the formation of some alcohol-induced neurological diseases. There are metabolic disturbances that are of equal importance, but these are more difficult to assess. Secondary nutritional problems also appear, such as infection, anemia and blood loss. All of these increase the individual's nutritional need.

Although alcohol-related illnesses of the nervous system are comparatively rare, when these diseases do appear, they seem to follow no definite pattern. They may appear in a relatively pure form, or they may appear in varying combinations. Sometimes one particular aspect is more pronounced, sometimes it is another. In many instances, individuals with the same characteristics react differently. One person may develop severe neurological symptoms while another may not.

It is always very difficut to isolate the cause of a particular disease in the chronic alcoholic. This is due to the complicating factors that appear when the system withdraws from alcohol. These frequently mask the more serious nutritional problems that might be present.

Wernicke-Korsakoff Syndrome: This pair of diseases, *Wernicke's encephalopathy* and *Korsakoff's syndrome* were mentioned earlier. But as they are so closely involved with the central nervous system, we feel it important to discuss them at greater depth in relation to neurological problems.

These diseases are generally regarded as two distinct clinical aspects of the same entity. They are the most common of the alcohol-nerve diseases and are caused by the same deficiencies. Their symptoms are frequently indistinguishable from each other.

Although usually associated with acute alcoholism these two diseases have been known to appear in non-alcoholics when severe nutritional deficiencies are involved. Most researchers accept the hypothesis that these diseases are caused by a profound lack of thiamin, or vitamin B_1.

The Wernicke-Korsakoff syndrome usually affects only those persons who have been drinking steadily for years. Its appearance may be abrupt. Its symptoms include mental confusion, ataxia, eye problems and various combinations of other nervous disorders. Interestingly enough, the patient may only complain of the ataxia, which is a condition of standing and walking difficulties. Frequently, the nerve problems are completely unnoticed.

The first indication that Wernicke-Korsakoff syndrome has appeared, may be a lack of spontaneity accompanied by apathy The patient may also lose his orientation in time and space and be unable to identify familiar objects and people.

As the patient's condition worsens, the symptoms become more evident. One of these is known as an *amnestic cofabulatory symptom*. It is a memory disorder that interferes with the higher cerebral functions. The ability to learn new things vanishes, as does the ability to remember recent events. Retrograde amnesia appears and the ability to form abstractions and concepts may be seriously impaired.

There is no set amount of time for recovering from these diseases. Some symptoms vanish as soon as treatment has begun, and some last longer. If vision has been seriously impaired, it may take weeks before the eyes return to normal. In severe cases, the eyes may not improve at all.

Ataxia improves slowly, if at all. In over half the patients who exhibit this symptom, the ability to walk and stand properly are permanently impaired. Permanent damage often results. Of 104 cases studied in 1971, only 21 per cent recovered completely. All 104 of these patients developed permanent amnesia when it came to questions concerning their illnesses; 25 per

119

cent showed significant improvement, but incomplete recovery; 28 per cent improved slightly; and 26 per cent were permanently afflicted. Periods of recovery varied from nine days to a year.

Wernicke-Korsakoff syndrome is nutritionally based. In a large number of cases, heavy alcohol use and inadequate dietary intake are common symptoms. Also, other indications of nutritional deficiency such as cirrhosis, anemia, lesions in the mucous membranes, loss of subcutaneous fat, and skin eruptions are frequently seen. Treatment consists of nutritional supplements and is usually successful, even when alcoholic ingestion is continued. Thiamin alone is effective in most cases. This supports the contention that the appearance of this disease is primarily due to an absence of thiamin.

A great deal is known about thiamin and its importance in maintaining the body's health. But we do not know how its absence causes nervous system dysfunction and the irreversible damage. Further research is needed.[1]

Cerebellar Cortical Degeneration: This syndrome is nutritionally based and most often appears in alcoholics under the age of fifty. Although it is frequently referred to as *alcoholic cerebellar degeneration,* it also appears in malnourished individuals who do not drink. There are, however, specific differences between the alcoholic form of the disease and the purely malnutritional one.

Frequently, the first symptom is ataxia. The patient complains of a progressive unsteadiness of gait and stance, which can become totally incapacitating. The arms seem to be affected less than the legs. Eye problems are also sometimes present as well as a slight trembling of the hands and slowed sleep patterns.

Generally, this disease develops rapidly, but not always. It reaches its maximum severity in a few days or weeks and then relative stability follows. Sometimes it is mild at the outset and becomes more severe when triggered by an illness in some other part of the body.

120

Treatment consists of nutritional supplements and abstention.

Again, the exact causes of this disease are not clear. It has been suggested that prolonged exposure to acetaldehyde might be a major factor, and this contention is supported by studies that have found acetaldehyde in all of the alcoholic's body organs, particularly the brain. This is further upheld by the fact that the administration of this chemical to humans and animals brings on attacks of ataxia.[5]

Amblyopia: This disease is sometimes called *tobacco-alcohol amblyopia.* However, as it is nutritional rather than the result of a toxic effect of the two substances, alcohol and tobacco, it might more properly be called *nutritional amblyopia.*

Amblyopia is a rare disorder of the eye. It usually appears in the confirmed alcoholic with a lengthy history of drinking problems.

The symptoms are associated with classic nutritional deficiency. They include weight loss, wasted muscles and subcutaneous tissue, and the thinness, coarseness and dryness of skin, among others. Many sufferers of this disease also exhibit liver damage and other manifestations of nervous system degeneration. Amblyopia is commonly found in only one out of every two hundred persons hospitalized for alcoholism, most commonly among men who also smoke.

The disease appears slowly. It begins with a slight vision impairment that gets progressively worse. Sometimes, several weeks may pass before the damage is really noticeable. Sometimes it is even a matter of months. Usually, the afflicted individual complains of a gradual blurring or dimness of vision. He will also frequently complain of a lack of ability to distinguish between certain colors, particularly red and green.

The syndrome is reversible with dietary supplements and an improvement in eating habits. Whether or not the patient stops drinking does not seem to affect the improvement rate. The length of time needed for the patient to respond to treatment is directly related to the length of time the disease has been evident before treatment is begun.

Although the origins of this disease are not clear, evidence points in the direction of some nutritional deficiency rather than some toxic effect of alcohol. As added support, there is another disorder which is indistinguishable from amblyopia and which has been observed in individuals with diabetes and vitamin B_{12} deficiency. This has been widely observed all over the world, particularly in countries where famine and drought prevail. In the more favored countries it has been observed only in alcoholics and those who otherwise neglect their nutrition.[3]

Central Pontine Myelinolysis: The principal symptoms of this rare disease are a progressive weakness in the bulbar muscles, an inability to swallow, and an absence of the gag reflex. It is generally seen in long-time alcoholics suffering from malnutrition, but it has also been seen in nonalcoholics who are malnourished.

Diagnosis of central pontine myelinolysis is difficult as the disease appears in a variety of ways. Normally, its presence is only firmly established after death. It often affects adults in the middle years, but it has also been seen in children.

As this disease progresses, the patient becomes drowsy, stuporous, and finally comatose. The duration of this progress is not clear as the difficulty encountered in diagnosis causes the moment of onset to be obscured. During the period of progression, the patient often dies from other complications — pneumonia, septicemia, uremia or urinary tract infection, among others.

The primary area of damage in this disease is the brain. This occurs in a group of nerve fibers called the *pons*.

There are two types of fibers in the pons, those running transversely, connecting the hemispheres of the brain, and those running longitudinally, connecting the *medulla* with the *cerebrum*. Lesions appear on these nerves and there is a pronounced destruction of the nerve sheath. This type of damage is also frequently observed in Wernicke's Disease, alcoholic cerebral degeneration and pellagra.

The source of this disease is not clear. As with so many nervous disorders that are thought to be alcohol induced, central pontine myelinolysis has not undergone systematic investigation. There are several interesting theories concerning this rare nerve disease, but there is still no conclusive evidence.[2]

Marchiafava-Bignami Disease: This disease was described in 1903 by Marchiafava and Bignami. It was then seen as a progressive, dementing illness associated with deterioration of the part of the brain known as the *corpus callosum*. It was first noticed in Italy among heavy drinkers of wine.

Until recently, only a few cases of this disease had even been studied; none when the disease was diagnosed before death. In 1956 researchers reported that Marchiafava-Bignami disease appears predominantly in middle-aged alcoholic males.

The development of the disease is erratic. It may take only a few days, and it may take several months. It has also been known to vanish suddenly, although this is rare. The symptoms include agitation, confusion, hallucinations of all types, memory disturbances, negativism, impaired judgment and disorientation. There are also other symptoms that suggest that other parts of the brain might be involved as well. These include language abnormality, disturbance of motor skills, seizures, brooding, gasping, sucking and an inability to initiate action.

The origins of this disease are unknown. It is certain, however, that it is a complication of chronic alcoholism. It has been seen in conjunction with Wernicke's disease and amblyopia, and its symptoms have been reported in

123

nonalcoholic, nutritionally deficient individuals. This would suggest that it is another case of alcoholic malnutrition.[1]

Pellagra: Pellagra is no longer a menace. This is mainly due to the fact that most people know enough about good nutrition to maintain sufficient dietary intake to prevent this disease. Most often today, pellagra is found among chronic alcoholics, particularly those who are also suffering from other nutritional complications. The symptoms resemble those of the encephalopathies, and there may be nerve and spinal-cord involvement.

One of the most obvious symptoms of pellagra is a condition that develops when the skin is exposed to the sun. This is not always the first symptom to appear, however. In the beginning, the patient usually complains of depression. This is frequently accompanied by apathy, fear, or apprehension. There may also be complaints of insomnia coupled with dizziness and headache. As the disease worsens, confusion, elusion, disorientation and hallucinations may also develop. Eventually the patient lapses into a coma. Treatment for pellagra consists of supplemental niacin, which generally causes a fast reversal.

Pellagra is attributed to a deficiency of nicotinic acid, or to a deficiency of tryptophan, one of the precursors of nicotinic acid.[4]

Alcoholic Dementia: This is a degenerative disease of the brain that produces confusion and profound memory loss. It is sometimes accompanied by leg spasticity, gait disturbance, fine picking movements, and tremulousness of the fingers and lips. In some individuals, a marked pallor of the optic disk can also be observed.

Many of the symptoms of alcoholic dementia are similar to those seen in Marchiafava-Bignami disease, and post-mortem brain examination frequently uncovers great damage. Some researchers even maintain that alcoholic dementia is not a separate disease but a further manifestation of the Marchiafava-Bignami syndrome.[1]

Summary: We have now become acquainted with some of the nerve diseases that are felt to be alcohol induced. Although these diseases may not be of great importance to the average reader, they have been included to inform and to underscore the nutritional dangers inherent in excessive drinking.

In the next chapter we will examine alcohol's effect on the liver, the organ most sensitive to alcoholic abuse.

REFERENCES AND ADDITIONAL READING FOR CHAPTER SIX

1. Dreyfus, P. M., "Diseases of the Nervous System in Chronic Alcoholics," *Biology of Alcoholism*, Volume 3, Clinical Pathology, 1974.
2. Adams, R. D., *et al.*, "Central Pontine Myelinolysis: A Hitherto Undescribed Disease Occuring in Alcoholic and Malnourished Patients," *Archives of Neurological Psychiatry*, 81:154, 1959.
3. Carroll, F. D., "Etiology and Treatment of Tobacco-Alcohol Amblyopia," *American Journal of Opthamalogy*, 27, 847, 1947.
4. Bean, W. B., *et al.*, "Incidence of Pellagra," *Journal of the American Medical Association*, 140:872, 1949.
5. Allsop, J., Turner, B., "Cerebellar Degeneration Associated with Chronic Alcoholism," *Journal of Neurological Science*, 3: 238, 1966.
6. Kissin, B., Kaley, M. M., "Alcohol and Cancer," *Biology of Alcoholism*, Volume 3, Clinical Pathology, 1974.
7. Greer, F. G., "Hypoglycemia of Hypo-Adrenocorticism and Alcoholism," *The Journal of Alcoholism*, Volume 7, No. 4, 1972.
8. "Alcoholic Myopathy," *The New England Journal of Medicine*, 1326, June 9, 1966.
9. Mayer, R. F., Garcia-Mullin, R., "Peripheral Nerve and Muscle Disorders Associated with Alcoholism," *Biology and Alcoholism*, Vol. 2, Chap. 2.
10. Song, S. K., Rubin, E., "Ethanol Produces Muscle Damage in Human Volunteers," *Science*, Vol. 175, 327-8, January 21, 1972.
11. French, S. W., "Acute and Chronic Toxicity of Ethanol: The Nervous System," *Biology of Alcoholism*, Vol. 1, Chap. 14, 1970.
12. Leevy, C. M., *et al.*, "Biochemistry of Gastrointestinal and Liver Disease in Alcoholism," *Biology of Alcoholism*, Vol. 1, Chap. 9, 1970.

13. Jellinek, E. M., "Nutritional Etiologies of Alcoholism," *The Disease Concept of Alcoholism*, College and University Press, New Haven, Connecticut, 1960.

14. Williams, H. L., Salamy, A., "Alcohol and Sleep," *Biology and Alcoholism*, Vol. 2, Chap. 13.

15. Mello, N. K., Behavioral Studies of Alcoholism: Sleep Patterns," *Biology and Alcoholism*, Vol. 2, Chap. 9.

16. "Martinis and Motherhood," *Newsweek*, July 16, 1973.

17. "Alcoholism Breeds Deformities," *Science Digest*, December, 1973.

18. Halsted, C. H., *et al.*, "Distribution of Ethanol in the Human Gastrointestinal Tract," *Am. J. Clin. Nutri,* 26: 831-34, 1973.

19. Mezey, E., *et al.*, "Pancreatic Function and Intestinal Absorption in Chronic Alcoholism," *Gastroenterology,* Vol. 59, No. 5, November, 1970.

20. Lorber, S. H., *et al.*, "Diseases of the Gastrointestinal Tract," *Biology and Alcoholism*, Vol. 3, Clinical pathology.

21. Van Thiel, D. H., Gavaler, J., Lester, R., "Ethanol Inhibition of Vitamin A Metabolism in the Testes: Possible Mechanism for Sterility in Alcoholics," *Science Digest*, Vol. 186, December 6, 1974.

22. Tuyns, A. J., "Cancer of the Esophagus: Further Evidence of the Relation to Drinking Habits in France," *Int. J. Cancer*, 5(1): 152, 1970.

23. Lamu, L., "Étude de Statistique Clinique de 134 Cas de Cancer de L'oesophage et du Cardia," *Arch. Mal. App. Dig.*, 4:451-475, 1910.

24. Rothman, K., Keller, A., "The Effect of Joint Exposure to Alcohol and Tobacco in Risk of Cancer of the Mouth and Pharynx," *J. Chron. Ds.*, 25:711-716, 1972.

25. Stenback, F., "The Tumorigenic Effect of Ethanol," *Acta Pathol Microbiol Scand.*, 77:325-326, 1969.

26. Dreher, K. F., Fraser, J. G., "Smoking Habits of Alcoholic Outpatients," *Int. J. Addict.*, 2(2): 259-270, 1962; 3:65-80, 1968.

27. Wynder, E. L., Pross, I. J., "A study of Etiological Factors in Cancer of the Esophagus," *Cancer,* 14:389-413.

127

28. Keller, A. Z., "The Epidemiology of Lip, Oral, and Pharyngeal Cancers and the Association with Selected Systemic Diseases," *Am. J. Pub. Health,* 53:1214-1228, 1965.
29. Schwartz, D., *et al.*, "Alcool et Cancer; Résultats d'une Enquête Rétrospective," *Revue Française d'Etude Clinique Biologique,* 7:590-604, 1962.
30. Pell, S., D'Alonzo, C. A., "A 5-Year Mortality Study of Alcoholics," *Journal of Occupational Medicine,* 15:120-125, 1973.
31. Hyrayama, T., "A Prospective Study on the Influence of Cigarette Smoking and Alcohol Drinking on the Death Rates on Total and Selected Causes of Death in Japan," *Smoke Signals,* 16(7):1-6, 1970.
32. Breslow, N. E., Endstrom, J. E., "Geographic Correlations Between Cancer Mortality Rates and Alcohol-Tobacco Sales in the United States," *Journal of the National Cancer Institute,* 1974.
33. Macdonald, W. C., "Clinical and Pathologic Features of Adrenocarcinoma of the Cardia," *Cancer,* 29:724-732, 1972.
34. Hodgkin, A. L., "Ionic Movements and Electrical Activity in Giant Nerve Fibers," *Procedures of the Royal Society, London Biologists,* 1958.
35. *First Special Report to U.S. Congress on Alcohol and Health from the Secretary of Health, Education and Welfare,* Department of Health, Education and Welfare, DHEW Publication 72-9099, December, 1971.
36. Jenkins, J. S., Connolly, J., "Adrenocortical Response to Ethanol in Man," *British Medical Journal,* 1968: 804, 1968.
37. Badr, F. M., Badr, R. S., *Nature,* Vol. 253, pp. 134-6.
38. "A Man's Drinking May Harm His Offspring," *Science News,* Vol. 107, February 22, 1975.
39. Segal, Julius, Luce, Gay Gaer, *Sleep,* Arena Books, New York, 1972.

CHAPTER SEVEN

ALCOHOL AND THE LIVER

It is in the liver that alcohol metabolism takes place. Because of this, the liver is the organ that is most prone to damage from alcoholic abuse. This chapter will attempt to clarify how the liver deals with alcohol and the possible consequences of overindulgence.

THE METABOLISM OF ALCOHOL

Alcohol does not require digestion. It moves directly into the bloodstream through the body tissue. As soon as an alcoholic beverage touches the lips the alcohol begins to move through the lining of the mouth and into the blood. Another minute portion of alcohol reaches the blood through the stomach lining. The rest passes into the intestines and is absorbed into the body through the lining of the small intestine.

Once in the blood in diluted form, the alcohol passes through the liver. It is there that metabolism takes place.

The first step in alcohol metabolism is its conversion into acetaldehyde. This is the first product of alcohol metabolism. It is produced when alcohol is exposed to the enzymes *alcohol dehydrogenase,* or ADH, and *nicotinamide-adenine dinucleotide,* or NAD. These enzymes are both produced by the liver.

Acetaldehyde is then converted into acetate, which is usable for energy. The final product of alcohol metabolism is carbon dioxide and water.

Excessive intake of alcohol produces striking imbalances in the liver. There are several reasons for this. First, there is only a limited amount of NAD available for use. Second, there is no feedback mechanism associated with alcohol metabolism, so the body is unable to adjust its rate of metabolism. These two factors account for serious consequences.

One of the most noticeable effects of excessive alcohol intake is the raised level of lactic acid in the blood. This slows the action of the kidneys and contributes to the condition known as *gout.* Alcohol is, therefore, a major factor in this condition.

THE RELATIONSHIP OF FAT METABOLISM TO ALCOHOL

Alcohol metabolization releases excessive amounts of hydrogen from the liver. In the event that large quantities are consumed, the *mitochondria,* the particles that produce energy, utilize hydrogen from alcohol rather than from fatty acids because the fat is more difficult to convert. In other words, instead of its normal function of burning fat, the liver burns alcohol. Since the available fat is not used, it accumulates in the liver. When insufficient fat is available in the diet, the body will manufacture it and that will be stored in the liver.

The liver disposes of fat by increasing its secretion of proteins into the blood. These are called *lipid-proteins. Lipid* is another term for excess fat. This causes *hyperlipemia,* a condition of mildly elevated fat content in the blood, which is usually associated with alcoholism. It becomes markedly exaggerated whenever diabetes, pancreatitis or other abnormalities in lipid metabolism are present.[18]

FATTY LIVER

Fatty liver appears when there is a breakdown in the mechanism controlling the movement of fat into the blood. When this happens, the fat can only accumulate. If this accumulation continues, the condition can only worsen.

Fat accumulation is the first damage to the liver caused by excessive alcohol. It seems to have no severe consequences, although minor problems have been reported. Sometimes a disease called *Choletatasis* develops, and in rare cases *jaundice* may appear. This condition is dangerous and can result in coma and death.

Fatty liver is usually reversible if the patient can remain abstinent.[14]

ALCOHOLIC HEPATITIS

This disease only appears after years of heavy drinking. It is an inflammatory disease, and its symptoms include fever, elevated white-cell count, pain in the upper right abdominal quadrant and jaundice. These symptoms frequently confuse researchers as they are quite similar to those encountered when the patient is suffering from gallstones. The most characteristic feature of alcoholic hepatitis must be observed under a microscope. It is called the *Alcoholic Hyalin of Mallory.* It is a form of cell degeneration, which with very few exceptions is endemic to alcoholic liver damage.

Alcoholic hepatitis usually subsides as soon as the patient gives up alcohol. It is potentially lethal, however, and there have been deaths reported in spite of discontinued alcoholic intake. This disease can develop into cirrhosis as drinking continues—but again, cirrhosis may appear in spite of abstinence. There is no consistent rule.[20]

CIRRHOSIS

Cirrhosis of the liver, in association with alcohol abuse, was first noticed in the last century by famous English researcher Dr. William Heberden. Since that time it has been proven that liver cirrhosis is directly attributable to alcohol consumption.

Cirrhosis of the liver is increasing alarmingly. In New York City, for example, cirrhosis is the third leading cause of death between the ages of twenty-five and sixty-five. Most of these deaths can be attributed to alcohol abuse.

As a general estimate, 10 percent of all alcoholics will develop cirrhosis if drinking continues long enough. This disease is disabling and potentially fatal. It is a scarring of the liver that impairs liver function. For once, we have a disease that, although alcohol related, does not seem to be nutritionally based. It correlates directly with the duration and quantity of alcohol consumption. In some cases, it causes iron to accumulate in the liver. This in turn may cause scar tissue to form that further complicates the cirrhosis. If the individual continues to drink he may die of portal hypertension or from total liver collapse.

Cirrhosis damage *cannot* be reversed. However, this does not mean that the individual is hopelessly ill. The prognosis improves if the individual abstains. The biggest complication that can result from the later stages of cirrhosis, even among individuals who have not taken alcohol for many years, is cancer of the liver.

There is yet another possible complication of alcoholic liver disease. This is *central sclerosing hyalin necrosis*. This syndrome involves scarring around the small veins in the liver. Those scars produce fibers that can enlarge to the point where they narrow or seal off the veins, causing a distortion in the shape of the liver. This leads to hypertension, even in cases where cirrhosis is not present.[16]

Alcoholic Liver Injury: The Mechanism: For many years, researchers assumed that alcoholic liver damage was associated with some toxic effect of the alcohol. In the 1930's this came under attack when it was noticed that many of the effects attributed to alcohol poisoning could also be attributed to malnutrition. In 1964, however, the original contention was upheld when it was proved conclusively that alcohol intake alone could produce fatty liver and the changes in liver cells which are seen in alcoholic hepatitis. This damage is present even when an adequate diet is maintained. And, it can appear after only *two days* of heavy alcohol ingestion.[15]

An interesting note is that liver damage can result from continuing ingestion of alcohol, even in amounts that do not produce inebriation. This has become particularly evident among individuals who drink a great deal in the course of their work, who function normally and who are not considered alcoholics. Such individuals, if they continue drinking consistently, increase the risk of liver damage considerably.

Although fatty liver is not an inflammatory disease, examination of tissue under the electron microscope shows a remarkable similarity between fatty liver damage and cirrhosis. This suggests that the fatty liver might be an earlier form of the more serious disease. This has not been proven, however, because it is difficult to induce cirrhosis in experimental animals.[15]

There is also evidence that fatty liver and cirrhosis are not connected. This is based on the fact that only a few alcoholics ever develop cirrhosis, while *all* alcoholics develop fatty liver.

Why cirrhosis develops in some alcoholics and not in others is not clear. It has been hypothesized that, in addition to the duration and amount of alcoholic consumption, there might be other related factors such as additives in alcoholic beverages, patterns of alcohol intake, genetic predisposition and malnutrition. Recently, a study was initiated that might show how cirrhosis is formed.

In the early 1970's Dr. Rubin and Dr. Lieber initiated a series of experiments in which baboons were made alcoholic.[21] Thirty-two baboons were used in this study. They were housed in separate cages and were initially fed on a high-protein biscuit diet.

Half of these baboons were given a 4 per cent alcohol solution, while the other half received water mixed with dextrinmaltose. All of these animals also received supplemental vitamins in more than sufficient amounts.

As the experiment progressed, the alcoholic animals began to develop fatty liver. The others did not. Then the amount of alcohol the baboons were receiving was increased, and an alcoholic liquid diet was provided that accounted for 50 per cent of the baboons' daily caloric need. In human equivalents this amounts to approximately one quart of whisky per day.

During the period of the study the animals all maintained their weight due to the nutritional elements they received. Of the sixteen animals in the control group, *none* developed liver disease. Of the alcoholic animals, *all* developed fatty liver, seven developed severe lesions, five developed alcoholic hepatitis, and two developed cirrhosis.

Three of the alcoholic baboons died after four years.

These deaths followed alcoholic withdrawal. This was an unavoidable complication as these baboons developed respiratory infections resulting in a loss of appetite. Autopsies on these three animals showed no visible damage to any part of the body except the liver. The two that developed cirrhosis exhibited symptoms identical to those seen in human beings with the disease.

Why didn't all of the animals develop cirrhosis? That question was considered by the researchers and their conclusion was that it is a matter of time. That is, given enough time, presumably all the other animals would develop the disease. This has been upheld by other studies that indicate development of cirrhosis is not only attributable to the consumption of alcohol but also to the length of time drinking continues.

The way cirrhosis develops still eludes us. We know that alcohol either favors the development of cirrhosis or in some way inhibits its remission. Patients who stop drinking usually live considerably longer than those who do not.

There are several important factors to be considered in light of the baboon study. The first is that a new type of animal model has been developed that might pave the way toward more extensive disease studies. The second is that the researchers have proved that alcohol alone—even when nutritional deficiency is not present, and even when the amount must be on the order of a quart of whisky a day over a period of many years—can produce alcoholic cirrhosis.

There is, of course, much controversy surrounding this issue. We have previously seen how alcohol affects the gastrointestinal tract by producing ulcers and electrical changes in the structure of the stomach lining. This keeps nutrition strongly in the minds of some researchers. They contend that the baboons did not receive adequate nutritional factors due to decreased absorption in the intestines.

Other researchers have also contradicted the conclusions of Drs. Lieber and Rubin. In one case, when rats were fed a diet where 50 per cent of the calories derived from alcohol, they did not develop fatty liver. It was felt that the rats were protected by a sufficiently nutritious diet.[22]

Still another challenge has come from researcher S. P. Lucia. He states that it is a matter of common sense that a quart of whisky a day might cause damage, but that this does not necessarily mean that alcohol itself is the cause. He maintains that enormous amounts of anything over a long period of time will cause some reaction—even if it is an essential nutrient.[23]

Regardless of all this, one fact remains clear; whatever the mechanism, whatever the actual origin of cirrhosis, alcohol is a contributing factor. Persons with no obvious nutritional deficiency may very well be victims of alcoholic hepatitis, which can develop into cirrhosis if drinking continues. It becomes then, important to discover if this disease is present in the body for cirrhosis is often fatal.

Summary: The first effect of alcohol on the body is the development of fatty liver. This can appear shortly after drinking commences. This is an accumulation of body fat in the liver that occurs when the liver loses the ability to transport fat into the blood. It is usually reversible if alcohol intake is stopped, but not always—this syndrome has caused sudden death.

Hepatitis is another form of alcohol-related disease that is more serious than fatty liver. The liver becomes inflamed and its structure is considerably altered.

The most serious condition is cirrhosis. If drinking is not stopped it can be fatal. No one knows exactly how cirrhosis develops, but some researchers feel that alcohol toxicity is to blame. Others claim that it is another example of alcoholic nutritional deficiency.

We have seen something of how alcohol is metabolized in the liver. We have briefly covered the action of *alcohol dehydrogenase* and its co-enzyme *nicotinamide-adenine dinucleotide*, how these two enzymes produce acetaldehyde and how this then breaks down into acetate, which is used for energy conversion.

REFERENCES AND ADDITIONAL READING FOR CHAPTER SEVEN

1. Leevy, C. M., "Metabolic and Nutritional Effects of Alcoholism," *Archives of Environmental Health*, Vol. 7, 1963.
2. Bourne, P. G., Fox, R., *Alcohol and Adrenocortical Function of Animals and Man*, New York Academic Press, 1973.
3. Shropshire, R. W., "The Hidden Faces of Alcoholism," *Geriatrics*, Vol. 30, No. 3, March, 1975.
4. Krasner, N., *et al.*, "Ascorbic Acid Saturation and Ethanol Metabolism," *Lancet*, Vol. 2, 1974.
5. Sprince, H., *et al.*, "Amino Acids, Vitamins Offset Acetaldehyde's Toxic Effects," *Medical Tribune*, Vol. 15, No. 19, 1974.
6. Sinclair, H. M., "Nutritional Aspects of Alcohol Consumption," *Procedures of the Nutritional Society*, 31, 117, 1972.
7. Jellinek, E. M., "Alcohol and Its Nutritional Significance," *Procedures of the Nutritional Society*, Vol. 14, 1955.
8. Eddy, T. P., "Alcoholic Beverages: A Neglected Factor in Dietetics," *Procedures of the Nutritional Society*, Vol. 32, No. 1, 1973.
9. Wilson, C. W. M., "The Pharmacological Actions of Alcohol in Relation to Nutrition," *Procedures of the Nutritional Society*, 31, 91, 1972.
10. Bebb, H. T., *et al.*, "Calorie and Nutrient Contribution of Alcoholic Beverages to the Usual Diets of 155 Adults," *American Journal of Clinical Nutrition*, Vol. 24, 1971.
11. Hartroft, W. S., "The Experimental Approach to Alcoholic Liver Damage," *Biological Basis of Alcoholism*, 1971.
12. Ugarte, G., Valenzuela, J., "Mechanisms of Liver and Pancreas Damage in Man," *Biological Basis of Alcohol*, 1971.

13. Takada, A., et al., "Regression of Dietary Cirrhosis in Rats Fed Alcohol and a Super Diet," *American Journal on Clinical Nutrition*, Vol. 20, No. 2, March, 1967.

14. Jones, D. P., "Influences of Dietary Fat on Alcoholic Fatty Liver," *American Journal on Clinical Nutrition*, Vol. 18, May, 1966.

15. Lieber, C. S., "Alcohol, Nutrition, and the Liver," *American Journal on Clinical Nutrition*, Vol. 26, No. 11, November, 1973.

16. Patrick, R. S., "Alcohol as a Stimulus to Hepatic Fibrogenesis," *Journal on Alcoholism*, Vol. 8, No. 1, 1973.

17. Lieber, C. S., "Quantitative Relationship Between Amount of Dietary Fat and Severity of Alcoholic Fatty Liver," *American Journal on Clinical Nutrition*, Vol. 23, No. 4, 1970.

18. Kudzma, D. J., "Alcoholic Hyperlipidemia: Induction by Alcohol But Not by Carbohydrate," *Journal of Laboratory Clinical Medicine*, March, 1971.

19. Linscheer, W. G., "Malabsorption in Cirrhosis," *American Journal on Clinical Nutrition*, Vol. 23, No. 4, April, 1970.

20. Beckett, A. G., et al., "Acute Alcoholic Hepatitis," *British Medical Journal*, 2:1113-1119, 1961.

21. Rubin, E., Lieber, C. S., "Fatty Liver, Alcoholic Hepatitis and Cirrhosis Produced by Alcohol in Primates," *New England Journal of Medicine*, 290:128-135, 1974.

22. Porta, E. A., et al., "Recovery from Chronic Hepatic Lesions in Rats Fed Alcohol and a Solid Super Diet," *American Journal on Clinical Nutrition*, 25:881-896, 1972.

CHAPTER EIGHT

ALCOHOL: Use and Misuse

ALCOHOL AND ADOLESCENCE

Most of the human studies cited in this book have had to do with adults. What about the large numbers of teenagers who drink? Many adults, even those who speak up loudly against marijuana and such substances, are surprisingly blasé when it comes to teenage drinking.

Teenage drinking is almost universal. A recent report from the Department of Health, Education and Welfare indicated that 93 per cent of twelfth-grade boys and 87 per cent of twelfth-grade girls have used alcohol. Twenty-three per cent of this number report getting drunk more than four times a year.[17] As far as most researchers are concerned, this is evidence of a drinking problem among a large number of teenagers that far surpasses marijuana use in terms of potential danger. This should not be surprising, of course. In view of the acceptance of drinking in the United States it is to be expected that the vast majority of teenagers have been introduced to alcohol.

Drinking increases with age. At first, beer is the most commonly imbibed form of alcohol, especially among boys. Beer drinking at least once a week is evidenced by 10 per cent of all seventh-grade boys studied. This incidence increases as the boys grow older until a frequency of once a week is established in 42 per cent of twelfth graders. Half of the boys studied reported drinking two or less drinks each time alcohol was available. Both girls and boys exhibit this increase as they grow older.[1]

Other drugs are not used as frequently. Marijuana, the great concern of the 60's has dropped to a poor second when compared with alcohol. Approximately 40 per cent of senior boys and 36 per cent of senior girls reported marijuana use. This is an average, of course. There are, naturally, regional variations. Southerners reported less use and Northeasterners reported more.

Drinking is heavier among students who also use marijuana. Ninety per cent of the marijuana users also drink while only 34 per cent of the drinkers also use marijuana.

The figures are lower in the case of hard drugs. Twelve per cent of senior boys studied had used hallucinogens and amphetamines, while less than 3 per cent had used heroin or cocaine.[1]

As is the case with other studies concerning alcohol use, it is extremely difficult to get a well-rounded picture of the situation. Many teenagers who drink heavily drop out of high school at an early age, thus making it difficult to obtain statistics on their drinking habits. The only dropouts who have been studied extensively are those who are spending time in correctional institutions. The few studies that have been conducted on the dropout population indicate that there are more drinkers in that group than in the group still enrolled in school. This means that teenage drinking may have been considerably underestimated.

Surveys show that among the teenagers who remain

in school, there is an increasing level of drinking. In one study, conducted between 1968 and 1973 by the San Mateo Department of Public Health and Welfare in San Mateo, California, it was found that in 1969, 52 per cent of seventh-grade boys were drinking. In 1973 this percentage had increased to 73 per cent.

The percentage of girls who drink increased similarly. In 1969 only 38 per cent of seventh-grade girls reported drinking. In 1973 this percentage had risen to 67 per cent.[9]

In the South there have been similar studies conducted with much the same results. These studies, completed in Florida in 1972, indicate that more students are drinking each year. Furthermore, the students who report drinking are drinking more frequently than their predecessors.[18]

In Toronto, Canada, three studies were undertaken; one in 1968, one in 1970 and one in 1972. In the first, 47 per cent of the students who responded indicated alcohol use within the preceding six-month period. In 1970 this percentage had increased to 60 per cent, and in 1972 the percentage had risen to 70 per cent.[19] These findings were amazingly consistent with those of the California study. It should be mentioned that during the period of the Canadian study, the drinking age was lowered to eighteen years. This does not seem to have been a factor in the increase, however, as the Florida study and the California study were conducted during the same period and the results were the same *without* a corresponding lowering of the drinking-age limit. This has also been upheld by studies in the New York area where the drinking age has been eighteen for many years.

These studies all indicate certain trends. Girls are using more alcohol in amounts often approaching boys, although not as many girls drink as boys. Drinking increases with age levels, and the number of children who start drinking seems to increase every year. The greatest increase was noted between 1970 and 1973.

Problem drinking in adolescence has no parallel among adults. There are too many different meanings and characteristics involved. By some standards, any adolescent who drinks has a problem. If getting high once a week is a criteria, then 5 per cent of our student population has a problem. Less conservatively, among those who get drunk four or more times a year, there are signs of problem drinking. It should be mentioned that this information was gathered on questionnaires that did not define "high" or "drunk"; the students themselves were allowed to define these concepts. In light of this, it is significant that only 2 per cent of the subjects responding felt that they might have a problem.

It is not surprising that juvenile delinquents show higher drinking levels than the general teenage population. This can be explained by the tendency of such individuals to misbehave in various ways, one of which is invariably drinking. For this reason, researchers feel in this case alcoholic intake is not an isolated problem but part of antisocial behavioral patterns.

These statistics give us some idea of the drinking patterns of teenagers. Statistics, however, cannot tell us why these patterns are emerging or why they are increasing at their current rate. In 1973 Dr. R. Jessor and his associates at the University of Colorado undertook a study designed to examine behavioral patterns that might contribute to excessive drinking in the teens.[20] Dr. Jessor reported that problem drinking is frequently associated with other types of misbehavior, much of which can be classified as deviant.

Problem drinkers consistently viewed achievement on any level as unimportant, while valuing independence above all else. Such drinkers were also more tolerant of deviant behavior than corresponding nondrinkers. It is interesting to note that girls who drink are less compatible with their parents than boys. It

144

is also not surprising that these teenage drinkers are highly in favor of drinking among adolescents.

Another study divided adolescents who drink into two major categories: the personally motivated student who does not use drugs or alcohol unless it is easily available; and the adolescent who is motivated by peer pressure. Among this latter group, parental pressure or permissiveness was a decided factor as to whether or not drinking occurred.[21]

Many feel that permissiveness is the major factor in teenage drinking. This is because drinking is relatively repressed in environments where alcohol is absolutely forbidden. This contention is not upheld by the evidence which indicates that problem drinking is more of a factor in areas where it is repressed than it is in areas where drinking is casually regarded.

One such study conducted at Mississippi State University showed a relationship between parental disapproval and increased drinking.[6] In another study it was found that drinking is less widespread at colleges which frown on drinking. At the same time, it was discovered that the highest percentage of drinkers who regularly get drunk are to be found in such institutions.[22]

Repressive situations then, may inhibit drinking among adolescents, however, at the same time, such a situation can be dangerous. It tends to bring teenagers with drinking problems into contact with one another. These adolescents drink together and are relatively isolated from their contemporaries. Thus, the social factors that usually keep drinking in check are not present and general difficulties may result.

Social factors that affect adolescent drinking are subject to special restrictions. First, teenagers begin drinking long before they can legally buy alcoholic beverages. This affects drinking patterns as well as the way in which alcohol is obtained. Most teenagers who drink begin at home, under parental control. This usually occurs during celebrations such as Christmas or Thanksgiving. As the teenager grows older, more drinking takes place outside the home until eventually there are no adults present at all.

In a 1974 study 60 per cent of seventh graders reported drinking in the home on special occasions. Only 22 to 36 per cent reported drinking outside the home. The interesting fact is that as the grade level increased, the number of students who reported drinking at home remained constant, while the number who reported drinking outside the home increased. For instance, the number of teenagers who drink at night while sitting in cars doubles between the ages of twelve and seventeen, while the number who drink at parties almost triples.[24]

THE ADULT POPULATION

We have seen that America is a drinking country. In 1965 it was found that 47 per cent of the adult population drink less than once a month, while 57 per cent drink more than that. In 1974 a survey of adults over the age of eighteen indicated that 68 per cent of the population regularly indulges in alcohol beverages. This is a 6 per cent increase over another survey conducted in 1969.[8]

Many factors apparently affect drinking patterns. Among these are age, ethnic background, religious affiliation, sex, educational level, economic status, occupation and area of residence.

Age: The highest level of abstinence can be found in the oldest age groups, while the highest percentage of drinkers can be seen in the group from twenty-one to twenty-four. This is not a complete picture, however, as the heaviest drinking takes place among males in the eighteen-to-twenty category.

A survey conducted in 1970 shed some interesting light on drinking among different age groups.[23] It was found that 67 per cent of the men who have been out of high school for one year drink once a month or more. Forty-four per cent drink once a week or more. Those who go into military service show higher levels than do those who remain in the civilian work force. In contrast, only 38 per cent of college freshmen report regular drinking. The men who enter military service not only show the highest level of drinking, but also report the highest percentage of changeover from abstinence to regular drinking. Among college students who participated in one 1971 survey, 60 per cent had drunk beer within the sixty-day period prior to the beginning of the study. Fifty-two per cent had drunk wine, while 49 per cent consumed spirits.

Religious Affiliation: It is a well-known characteristic of certain religious sects that abstinence is regarded as an ideal. In some, it is a requirement for membership. In others it is particularly encouraged. As we have seen earlier, religious groups have always been far more successful than legislators at regulating drinking. This is why alcohol use among churchgoers is an interesting field of study.

Catholics show the highest level of drinking among the three major religions. Those of Jewish descent evidence the lowest proportion of heavy drinkers as well as the lowest proportion of abstainers. Jews who drink are usually light drinkers.[25]

Liberal Protestants show patterns of drinking quite similar to Catholics as far as numbers are concerned. They do not seem to have as many heavy drinkers, however. Conservative Protestants show the highest percentage of total abstainers and the lowest percentage of heavy drinkers. One survey, conducted in 1972-74, indicates that there is a steady increase among Jews and Catholics as far as both light and moderate drinking is concerned. Protestants, on the other hand, have remained consistent over the years. It should be noted, however, that since 1965, when this survey was conducted, the number of people who claim no religious affiliation has more than doubled.[25]

Religious affiliation and drinking in adolescents has also been studied. As in the case of adults, the amount of involvement with church activities has a great deal to do with drinking patterns.[26]

Sex: In the adult population 60 per cent of women drink as compared with 77 per cent of the men.[25] In addition the proportion of women drinkers has increased steadily since World War II. Forty-seven per cent of adult women drink once a month or more. Men are still the heaviest drinkers, however, and it is twice as likely that a man will become a moderate drinker than a woman. Among women, heavy drinking is most likely to occur between the ages of twenty-one and twenty-nine.[27]

Educational Level: This is a major factor in alcohol consumption. It is believed that most abstainers have less than an eighth-grade education. The proportion of heavy drinkers apparently increases from that point consistently. Six per cent of those with grammar school educations are heavy drinkers, compared with 10 per cent of those who have undergone post-graduate training.[28]

Economic Status: Individuals in the lower economic strata seem to be abstainers more often than those in the higher levels. Recent surveys uphold this theory, as well as the fact that moderate and heavy drinking is more prevalent among the upper economic strata.[28]

This seems to hold true in the case of adolescents as well. In one recent study in Toronto, Canada, it was found that high school students whose fathers are among the professional or managerial classes show the highest alcohol use.[29] These findings were upheld by a study conducted at the University of Michigan's Institute for Social Research. This latter study also indicated that wealthier adolescents increase their alcohol use by a full 21 per cent after leaving high school; this, in contrast to only a 5 per cent increase among the poorer classes.[23]

Occupation: Occupations account for a wide variety of drinking patterns. In 1969 a study was completed at the Rutgers Center for Alcoholic Studies in New Brunswick, New Jersey. It indicated that farm owners and residents of rural areas show the largest proportion of drinkers. In contrast, professionals and businessmen seem to drink more heavily. Among those in the semi-professional classes, it is believed that those who do drink tend to become heavy drinkers.[25]

In 1972 a survey was undertaken in Princeton, New Jersey, with almost 550 executives in the five-hundred largest manufacturing companies in the United States. It also included fifty of the largest banks, transportation industry organizations, utilities, life insurance companies, and merchandising organizations. The results of this study were revealing. Only 7 per cent of those participating were abstainers, or drank less than once a month. In contrast, 32 per cent in the general population abstain. Among the executives studied, the proportion of heavy drinkers was considerably lower than among the general population. Thirteen per cent were classified as heavy drinkers, as opposed to 21 per cent in the general population. Forty-eight per cent of these executives were moderate drinkers, but 17 per cent felt they should cut down on their drinking.[30]

In 1973 a new study compared drinking patterns with alcoholism among blue collar workers. This survey seemed to indicate that there are *fewer* drinkers, *heavier* drinkers, and more of what might be termed *heavy-escape* drinkers among blue collar workers than among other groups. Twenty-three per cent of the women in this group drink. Of these, a full 38 per cent can be classified as heavy or problem drinkers.[31]

In 1972 two individual surveys were conducted for the Department of the Army[5] and the Bureau of Naval Personnel.[4] They supported the contention that military

149

men, both officers and enlisted men, tend to be heavy drinkers. In addition, enlisted men seem to get into more trouble because of their drinking habits than do their civilian counterparts. It is interesting to note that enlisted men continue to drink heavily throughout their military careers even though heavy drinking and problem drinking decline as age increases and rank is obtained.

Very few members of the armed forces are thought to be abstainers and only 3 per cent of enlisted men in the Army and 4 per cent of the officers. The situation is the same in the Navy.

Residence: Drinking patterns vary from geographical area to geographical area. There are apparently more drinkers in New England and the Middle Atlantic and coastal states than there are in the Southern states.[25] These regional contrasts can be partially explained by the fact that the Northern states and the Pacific Coast states are more highly urbanized than the Southern states. It should be noted, however, that this situation seems to be changing. In the Southeast and Rocky Mountain states, which have been considered light drinking areas, heavy drinking is increasing.[28] Why this is happening is not clear. Drinking habits in these states may indeed be changing. However, the difference in drinking habits might reflect the highly mobile life style of many Americans today.

Small cities and towns contain more abstainers. In large cities and suburbs the drinking rate is almost double that of rural areas.

What social pressures cause people to drink? For most, the presence of family and friends is necessary for drinking to be enjoyable. Indeed, the term "social drinking" would seem to indicate that most drinking patterns are determined by the social climate of our lives. It is an activity in which most people can participate and in which there is normally no competition. It might be said that drinking is a leveler—it puts people at their ease, and it helps them relax and enjoy the companionship of their fellows.

One study showed that Americans tend to drink more heavily in their homes than they do in restaurants and bars. This has been upheld by later studies.[28]

It is well known that drinking behavior is influenced to a great degree by the people one drinks with. For instance, most people report that they drink more when they are with close friends than they do at social meetings that might include neighbors. It is interesting to note that even the type of beverage consumed is sometimes controlled by environmental conditions. For instance, distilled spirits are considered to be a party drink; beer is usually drunk in working situations or at athletic events.[25]

In the age group from eighteen to twenty-nine, drinking in bars, restaurants and taverns is most likely to take place. Women, however, do not drink as often in public places as men. Women of all ages tend to do their drinking at parties or on special occasions.[25]

Summary: The number of adults who drink more than once a month is rising. Sociological factors such as age, ethnic background, sex, religion, educational level, occupation and other socioeconomic reasons are apparently the major factors controlling whether a person drinks and if so how much. Regional differences in drinking patterns still exist, but recent studies seem to indicate that this is changing.

Problem drinkers are generally thought to be members of the less affluent classes. They tend to live in cities and many have moved from rural areas to large population centers.

ALCOHOL AND THE AGED

Abstinence is common among older people. Some give up drinking for health reasons, while others have been lifelong abstainers. An interesting note is that healthy and more active older people are more likely to be drinkers. Heavy drinking is rarely a problem of old age, for old age rarely becomes a problem for heavy drinkers. There are, of course, some individuals who begin to drink as they grow older for reasons directly connected with aging. This, together with the fact that the older population is growing, indicates that alcoholism among older people might someday become a problem.[15]

In one study conducted at the Rutgers Center for Alcoholic Studies in 1969 it was found that many individuals decrease their alcohol consumption as they age. This might indicate that alcoholism might tend to vanish as a person grows older. This is upheld by many well-documented studies indicating that many problem drinkers become abstainers or at least modify their drinking as they grow older.[25]

Only recently has alcoholism research begun to focus on the older age groups. In the last few years there have been three major research projects that have addressed themselves to alcohol and the elderly. The first surveyed drinking habits and patterns among a group of older persons living in New York City.[15] The second was a series of studies designed to outline major drinking studies in the elderly.[12] The third concerned the psychological and physiological results of introducing social drinking into a nursing home.[13] As a result of these three studies, we now have an excellent picture of the drinking habits of senior citizens.

At all ages, men drink more than women. It was not until these studies were undertaken that it was ascertained that heavy drinking usually decreases after the age of forty-nine in both sexes. An additional decline often occurs after age sixty-four. The number of women who abstain after the age of forty-nine also increases.

Among elderly abstainers it was found that half of the men aged sixty and over were former drinkers. Almost half of these had stopped drinking after the age of forty-four. Among women aged sixty and over, most of those who were abstainers had never been drinkers, but at least half of those who had, stopped after the age of forty-four.

It should be mentioned that drinking patterns among elderly people today will very likely not correlate with the elderly in the future. This can be explained by the various cultural patterns that influenced today's older persons in their youth and middle age. Many of these persons lived through the period of national prohibition. In addition, many who took up drinking as a rebellion in their youth, returned to abstinence as they aged. It will be several generations before we know whether or not abstinence among older persons can be accounted for by early conditioning.

Effects: Physical and Psychological: As mentioned earlier, there is no direct evidence that alcohol in moderate amounts is damaging. It may even be beneficial. There are statistical indications that persons who drink moderately live longer than abstainers. If this is the case it seems probable that these beneficial effects might particularly apply to the elderly.

It is unfortunate that so little information is available on the effects of excessive alcohol consumption on older people. There is evidence to suggest, however, that any beneficial effects of alcohol in moderate amounts might be due more to psychological than physical factors. For example, there is widespread belief that alcohol is beneficial to the heart and circulatory system. While there is no conclusive evidence for this, the psychological factors involved may be of great benefit.

In the New York study, questions were asked that were designed to discover why elderly people give up alcohol. Many former drinkers indicated that they had stopped drinking because they had felt that alcohol was making them ill, or that it might be bad for their health as they aged. In many cases researchers were able to detect a certain fear among these subjects that alcohol

153

might contribute to a gradual loss of physical and mental control. As this fear is always present to some degree in older persons due to the unavoidable disabilities of old age, their reasons for abstinence might be considered psychological.

In the study that introduced moderate amounts of alcohol in the nursing home environment, one group received beer in a bar setting. There was a marked behavioral improvement when comparisons were made with a control group receiving only orange juice in the same setting. In a similar study, patients received either beer or wine in the bar setting for a four-week period. In both cases there was a marked improvement in the attitude of the patients.

Summary: Although studies concerning the effects of alcohol on elderly persons are in short supply, enough evidence exists to lead us to several conclusions. Alcohol is consumed most often by older persons who are socially active and who consider themselves to be in good health. This is true whether the individual is institutionalized or not. There is no evidence that alcohol in moderate amounts is dangerous. There is even some indication that the psychological benefits of moderate drinking might outweigh the possible dangers. Many older individuals prefer alcohol as an attractive alternative to sedatives and other medication.

Although problem drinking does occur among older persons, it is quite clear that alcoholism is considerably less of a problem than it is among younger people. And their reasons for drinking are directly related to the physical and mental difficulties of aging.

REFERENCES AND ADDITIONAL READING FOR CHAPTER EIGHT

1. Bacon, M., Jones, M. B., *Teenage Drinking*, Crowell, New York, 1968.
2. Blacker, E., *et al.*, "Drinking Behavior of Delinquent Boys," *Quarterly Journal on the Studies in Alcohol*, 26: 223-237, 1965.
3. Calahan, D., *Problem Drinkers*, Jossey-Bass, San Francisco, 1970.
4. Calahan, D., Cisin, I. H., *Report of a Pilot Study of the Attitudes and Behavior of Naval Personnel Concerning Alcohol And Problem Drinking*, Bureau of Naval Personnel, Bureau of Social Science Research, Inc., Washington, D.C., February, 1973.
5. Calahan, D., *et al.*, *Drinking Practice and Problems in the U.S. Army*, Final Report of a Study Conducted for the Deputy Chief of Staff, Personnel, Headquarters, Department of the Army, December, 1972.
6. Globetti, G., *A Survey of Teenage Drinking in Two Mississippi Communities*, Mississippi State University, Social Science Research Center, State College, Mississippi, 1964.
7. Lolli, G., *et al.*, *Alcohol in Italian Culture: Food and Wine in Relation to Sobriety Among Italians and Italian Americans*, Rutgers Center of Alcohol Studies, New Brunswick, New Jersey, 1958.
8. Room, R., Beck, K., "Survey Data on Trends in U. S. Consumption," social research group working paper f. 27., School of Public Health, University of California, Berkeley, California, 1974.
9. San Mateo County Department of Public Health and Welfare, *Surveillance of Steady Drug Use*, San Mateo County, California, 1973.
10. Smart, R. S., Fejer, D., White, J., *Drug Use Trends Among Metropolitan Toronto Students: A Study of Changes from 1968 to 1972*, Addiction Research Foundation, Toronto, Canada, 1972.

11. Blane, H. T., "Preliminary Descriptive Data Tabulations for Irish-American and Italian American Drinking Practices Project," unpublished paper, January, 1974.

12. Carruth, B., *et al.*, "Alcoholism and Problem Drinking Among Older Persons," report submitted to Administration on Aging, Department of Health, Education and Welfare, Washington, D.C., 1974.

13. Chien, C. P., "Psychiatric Treatment for Geriatric Patients: Pub or Drug?", *American Journal of Psychiatry*, 127:1070-1075, 1971.

14. Drew, L. R. H., "Alcoholism as a Self-limiting Disease," *Quarterly Journal on the Studies in Alcohol*, 29:956-967, 1968.

15. Johnson, L. A., *Use of Alcohol by Persons 65 Years and Over, Upper East Side of Manhattan*, National Institute on Alcohol Abuse and Alcoholism, January, 1974.

16. Rosin, A. J., Glatt, M. M., "Alcohol Excess in the Elderly," *Quarterly Journal on the Studies in Alcohol*, 32:53-59, 1971.

17. *Second Special Report to the U. S. Congress on Alcohol and Health*, from the Secretary of Health, Education and Welfare, Washington, D.C., June, 1974.

18. *Student Drug and Alcohol Opinionaire and Usage Survey*, Duval County School Board, Jacksonville, Florida, 1972.

19. Smart, R. G., *et al.*, "Drug Use Trends Among Metropolitan Toronto Students: A Study of Changes from 1968 to 1972," Substudy #512, Addiction Research Foundation, Toronto, Canada, 1972.

20. Jessor, R., Jessor, S. L., *Problem Drinking in Youth: Personality, Social and Behavioral Antecedents and Correlates*, Publication #144, Institute of Behavioral Science, University of Colorado, Boulder, Colorado, 1973.

21. Braucht, G. N., *A Psychosocial Typology of Adolescent Alcohol and Drug Users*, Department of Health, Education and Welfare, Publication #75-137, Washington, D.C., 1974.

22. Straus, R., Bacon, S. D., *Drinking in College*, Yale University Press, New Haven, Connecticut, 1953.

23. Johnson, L., *Drugs and American Youth*, University of Michigan Institute for Social Research, Ann Arbor, Michigan, 1973.

24. Plaut, T. F. A., *Alcohol Problems: A Report to the Nation by the Cooperative Commission of the Study of Alcoholism*, Oxford University Press, New York, 1967.

25. Calahan, D., *et al.*, *American Drinking Practices: A National Study of Drinking Behavior and Attitudes*, Monograph #6, Rutgers Center of Alcohol Studies, New Brunswick, New Jersey, 1969.

26. Maddox, G. L., McCall, B. C., *Drinking Among Teenagers: A Sociological Interpretation of Alcohol Use by High School Students*, Monograph #4, Rutgers Center of Alcohol Studies, New Brunswick, New Jersey, 1964.

27. *First Special Report to the U. S. Congress on Alcohol and Health from the Secretary of Health, Education and Welfare*, U. S. Department of Health, Education and Welfare, Publication #73-9031, Washington, D.C., 1971.

28. Harris, L., *et al.*, *Public Awareness of a National Institute on Alcohol Abuse and Alcoholism Advertising Campaign and Public Attitudes Toward Drinking and Alcohol Abuse*, Overall Summary prepared for the National Institute on Alcohol Abuse and Alcoholism, 1974.

29. De Lint, J., Schmidt, W., "Consumption Averages and Alcoholism Prevalence: A Brief Review of Epidemiological Investigations," *British Journal on Addiction*, 66:97-107, 1971.

30. *Executive Knowledge, Attitudes and Behavior Regarding Alcoholism and Alcohol Abuse*, Caravan Surveys, Inc., Report prepared for National Institute on Alcohol Abuse and Alcoholism, January, 1972.

31. Siassi, I., *et al.*, "Drinking Patterns and Alcoholism in a Blue Collar Population," *Quarterly Journal on the Study of Alcoholism*, 24:917-926, 1973.

CHAPTER NINE

CHAPTER NINE

SOME ANSWERS TO THE PROBLEM

So far we have examined many of the effects and reasons for the consumption of alcohol. In discussing treatment for individuals with alcohol problems, we are confronted with many confusing factors. We do not know what causes alcoholism. We do not know if it is genetic or psychological or both. We do know that the greatest cause of illness and disease among alcoholics is nutritional imbalance. Many researchers seeking a treatment for alcoholism use this as a starting point and recommend megavitamin therapy. Other researchers consider the problem of alcoholism controllable by such controversial methods as bio-feedback and transcendental meditation. Still others consider chemical treatment the obvious answer.

Let us examine these various treatments, their methods and benefits.

There are as many methods of treating alcoholism as there are researchers. We feel that a nutritional approach is by far the most sensible. However, in order to give a well-balanced picture of the types of treatments used for alcoholism, several possible alternatives will be discussed.

Alcoholics are generally treated in one of two ways:

Some treatment centers specialize in only one type of treatment. Conditioned-reflex treatments, or behavior modification such as that involved by the use of the drug Disulfiram, better known as Antabuse, are espoused by many of these. Group therapy or psychodrama have also been used to great effect. Unfortunately, these treatments can be of no use unless the individual concerned is susceptible to the methods.

The second type of treatment uses a variety of methods—religious counseling, lectures, psychotherapy, and, in many cases, Alcoholics Anonymous. The basis for this approach is, "something has got to work." In some cases it does. But in others it might not.

Both types of treatment have come under criticism. In the first instance, the time is totally wasted if the patient does not respond to the particular treatment involved. In the second instance, time and human resources may be wasted as various approaches are tried that may prove ineffective. The question of which treatment for which patient is further complicated by the fact that alcoholics have nothing in common except their misuse of alcohol.

PHYSIOLOGICAL METHODS

Antabuse: One treatment for alcoholism that is receiving considerable support at this time concerns the drug Antabuse. This was first tried by Dr. Eric Jacobsen in Denmark in 1948. It is usually administered in a tablet containing half a gram of the drug. In the system, Antabuse causes a buildup of *acetaldehyde*.

Antabuse is first administered for several days under carefully controlled conditions. The patient is then given a small amount of an alcoholic beverage. The presence of Antabuse in the body causes a severe reaction. It becomes hot; nausea and vomiting occur, along with a sudden drop in blood pressure; the heart pounds and some individuals experience a feeling of impending death.

It thus becomes clear to the patient that he or she will be in extreme discomfort if alcohol is taken while Antabuse medication continues. Generally speaking, this experience is severe enough to keep the patient away from alcohol for quite some time. During the abstinence period, psychological and rehabilitative measures are undertaken which, it is hoped, will be effective in preventing the patient's return to alcohol after drug therapy is discontinued.

Naturally, this approach is negative. It is a form of aversion therapy that is itself condemned in many circles. There can be no doubt, however, that many alcoholics have been helped by this method.

Lithium: Until recently it was felt by most researchers that in order for an alcoholic to remain cured he or she must never take alcohol. This view is strongly supported by members of Alcoholics Anonymous, a group that has been extremely effective in the treatment of alcoholics. Within the past few years, however, a new substance has appeared that may change this approach. By all indications it is a drug that will permit alcoholics to become social drinkers by bringing about a chemical change in their systems. This drug is called *Lithium,* a common metallic salt.

The recovery rate of alcoholics has always been low. It is estimated that only one out of twenty alcoholics can succeed in rehabilitating themselves. With the advent of Lithium, however, there seems to be considerable new hope.

The discovery that Lithium might be valuable in the treatment of alcoholism was made almost accidentally. Initially, the researchers involved did not set out to discover a treatment for alcoholism. They were intrigued by the effects this antidepressant might have on normal human beings. The first in-depth study of Lithium was conducted by Dr. Nathan S. Kline, Director of Research of the Rockland State Hospital in Orangeburg, New York.

Until this study, Lithium was used only in the treatment of recurrent depression in psychiatric patients. It seemed to be particularly effective in the treatment of manic depression. Dr. Kline was initially intrigued by the evidence that suggested Lithium causes a change in the functioning of the thyroid gland. It was this change that Dr. Kline wished to study. The question raised was this: Does thyroid readjustment take place in normal individuals or only in those suffering from psychiatric disorders? The problem of immediate concern was to justify administering Lithium to normal persons for extended periods.

Earlier Dr. Kline had experimented with the antidepressant properties of Lithium and narcotics addiction. He found it to be effective in preventing recurrent patterns of addiction, and therefore theorized that many addicted individuals are essentially depressed. This same theory applies equally well to alcoholics. Dr. Kline felt it might be useful to administer Lithium to patients suffering from alcoholism.

The study took place at the Veterans Administration Hospital in Togus, Maine. This site was chosen because it is completely isolated, being the only hospital in a hundred-and-fifty-mile radius. This meant that alcoholics living in the immediate area could only be treated in one place; the Veterans Administration facility. So, an individual patient prone to recurring alcoholic bouts would turn up at the same hospital again and again, making the study easy to control.

The subjects were divided into two groups—the first receiving Lithium, the second, a placebo. All of the subjects were known to be heavy drinkers of spirits. They were described by Dr. Ervin Varga, a researcher at Rockland State Hospital, as "hard-core, treatment-resistant, chronic alcoholics who have been trying to stop drinking for quite some time." The ages of the subjects ranged from twenty-five to sixty-five, with the average age being in the mid-forties. Over half of these individuals were either separated or divorced.

The study began with a detoxification period. After approximately one month, the patients were discharged after being supplied with either Lithium or the placebo tablet. They were then directed to return to the hospital once a month for a physical examination. Naturally, due to the inconsistent behavior of most alcoholics, some of the subjects were lost at this point. This was mainly due to the failure of the individual concerned to take the medication.

In the beginning there were seventy-three patients involved in the study. After a year had passed, only thirty remained. After the end of two years, only twenty-one patients were returning to the hospital on a regular basis. This high attrition rate was not unexpected. It is a situation familiar to anyone conducting research among alcoholics. However, in this case it was not important, for those who remained with the study made dramatic progress after the first year on the medication. The number of disabling drinking bouts were markedly reduced in all of the patients receiving Lithium. Only 25 per cent of the Lithium patients were experiencing disabling drinking bouts after the first year, while a full 64 per cent of the control group were subject to this type of behavior. In addition those individuals receiving the placebo were consistent about the number of drinking bouts they experienced both before and after their hospitalization. In contrast, the Lithium group experienced only one-fourth the number of drinking bouts they had experienced before taking the drug. After the second year on the Lithium therapy, the results were even more dramatic. Only two of the patients on Lithium had had any drinking episodes whatsoever.

The most striking feature of Lithium treatment is its ability to allow an individual to continue drinking on a moderate scale. Most of these persons had followed a well-organized routine. They would work hard and maintain family relationships for weeks and months at a time. Then, very suddenly, they would drop out of sight and go on drinking binges until they would have to be hospitalized. Naturally, some of the patients in Dr. Kline's experiments did stop drinking, but this was not a typical response. The majority of the subjects did not stop taking alcohol, but the manifestations of alcoholism—delirium tremens, severe behavior and unconsciousness—became extremely rare. Commonly the patients reported, "I just feel better and I don't need to drink the way I did before." These once-hopeless alcoholics could now drink on a social level without the compulsion to get drunk.

Dr. Kline summed up this study with the statement, "Lithium seems to act on the compulsive aspect of drinking." Dr. Kline feels that Lithium might be the answer for other alcoholics who exhibit the binge-drinking syndrome.

Lithium is a safe drug when taken under medical supervision. In no case did an individual react adversely. There were one or two instances of mild gastrointestinal disturbance, and several patients reported a fine tremor of the hand. Lithium therapy must be maintained by continuous medication. Continuous treatment over a period of fifteen years or more has been recorded without any mention of deterioration in the condition of the patient.

Lithium is taken orally, in doses of three capsules a day. It is not an expensive drug as it is a natural element. Therefore, the only cost involved in making Lithium available is in the processing.

It is hoped that Lithium treatment can significantly change the lives of many millions of Americans who are currently addicted to alcohol. It also offers hope for countless relatives and employers as it indicates that this problem can be brought under control and those affected individuals can be returned to an active role in their societies.

Aversion Therapy: Aversion therapy is a method of creating a conditioned reflex in the form of an aversion to alcohol by causing the patient to become nauseated whenever alcohol is taken. This type of drug therapy associates extreme sickness and vomiting with drinking. The alcoholic develops a dislike for the smell, taste, and even the sight of alcoholic beverages.

Aversion therapy of any sort is condemned in many circles. For one thing, it is not permanent and must be periodically reinforced.

Other methods besides drugs can be used in aversion therapy. One method consists of administering a series of painful electric shocks to the subject when drinking is attempted. Again, this is an extremely negative approach and is not useful in all cases.

NUTRITION

The importance of nutrition cannot be overemphasized. Continually we have seen that it is nutrition more than any other factor that affects the health of alcoholics. It is a prime consideration if one is to overcome the effects of alcoholism. Nutritional factors must be rebalanced before the general health will improve.

The nutritional requirements of alcoholics are extremely exacting, and must be carefully watched. Unfortunately, due to the great variance from individual to individual, it is impossible to suggest one single effective diet for every alcoholic. There are, however, certain general principles that may be used as a guide.

First, any adequate diet must contain large quantities of high-quality protein. This is found predominantly in fish, red meat, poultry, milk, eggs and cheese. The average adult male requires approximately two to five ounces of protein each day. One pound of steak will provide this amount, as will ten ounces of cheese, ten medium eggs, or eight glasses of milk. There are other types of foods that also contribute protein to the diet such as beans, whole-grain cereals, and nuts. The inclusion of any of these cannot help but be beneficial.

While obtaining the necessary high-quality protein from the foods mentioned above, the alcoholic will obtain many of the vitamins and minerals which are necessary to good health. Dairy products are particularly effective in providing these as are vegetables and fresh fruits. Certain vegetables, such as broccoli, carrots and cabbage are of particular value as they contain large amounts of calcium. Vitamin A is available from most of the yellow vegetables.

Basic foods are the most nutritious. They contain the necessary nutriments needed for a complete diet. This is not true of many of the overly refined foods generally eaten in our society. These replace necessary elements in much the same way as alcohol does. Therefore, if excessive amounts of refined foods are included in the alcoholic's diet, they will satisfy the appetite without providing nutrition.

When dealing with alcoholics, it is frequently necessary to include vitamin supplements. This is especially true since it is so difficult to convince many alcoholics that they must eat properly on a continual basis. The following vitamin supplements are recommended on a daily basis:

Thiamin (B_1)	3.30mg.
Riboflavin (B_2)	2.67mg.
Nicotinamide	20.00mg.
Calcium pantothenate (B_3)	20.00mg.
Pyridoxin	3.30mg.
Biotin	0.05mg.

Folic acid	1.10mg.
p-Aminobenzoic acid	11.00mg.
Inositol	53.00mg.
Choline	53.00mg.
Vitamin B_{12}	5.00mg.
Vitamin A	6,667.00 units
Vitamin C.	66.70mg.
a-Tocopherol	6.67mg.
Viosterol	333.00 units
Lipoic acid	0.10mg.

This supplementary list is not complete. It is very difficult, given the cost of some nutritional elements, to provide a totally adequate supplementary dietary package. This is why it is so important to eat correctly. These supplements however, can be of invaluable aid.

The following additional mineral supplements are also recommended:

Manganese	5.00mg.
Molybdenum	0.20mg.
Zinc	5.00mg.
Cobalt	0.05mg.
Iron	10.00mg.
Iodine	0.05mg.
Copper	2.00mg.

PSYCHOLOGICAL METHODS

Bio-feedback: Recently, a new approach to an ancient discipline has captured a great deal of attention in the scientific world. This is known as bio-feedback.

The history of science is full of instances in which ancient techniques are found to have a solid scientific foundation. Such a technique is meditation—and its modern counterpart, bio-feedback.

Bio-feedback is a method of mental training that allows the individual to achieve conscious control over

167

the inner workings of the body. You may think that you already have conscious control of your body, but this is not true. Granted, to a certain degree, the conscious mind does control the more obvious physical processes; the use of the major motor systems, etc. It is the autonomic nervous system, however, that is responsible for controlling all of those processes that enable us to live healthy lives.

There are two nervous systems in the human body and their functions are quite different. The first is called the central nervous system. It is under the control of the conscious mind and affects the skeletal structure, the muscles, the joints and the limbs. This system utilizes thirty-two nerves that run down the spinal cord and into the body. This system also includes the conscious brain and the twelve pairs of nerves that control its impulses. The other system, the one with which we are most concerned when discussing bio-feedback, is known as the autonomic nervous system. Its control nerves also run along the spinal cord but regulate the functioning of the body within the skeletal frame; the internal organs, such as the stomach, the liver, the pancreas; the endocrine, or secreting glandular system; the respiratory system; the circulatory system; and millions of small muscles associated with organs such as the eyes and the nose.

The Autonomic System: Basically, bio-feedback provides a method in which the body can be completely controlled by the autonomic nervous system. This is not a new idea. It is almost as old as man himself. It is one which has surfaced in many of the Eastern and a few Western religions.

Is the autonomic nervous system capable of learning? The first evidence that this might be true came about through experiments conducted by Dr. Neal E. Miller at Rockefeller University in New York. Dr. Miller's experiments had to do with rats whose skeletal muscular systems had been paralyzed with the drug curare. By using this drug, Dr. Miller was able to reduce his subject animals to a condition in which they were totally incapable of utilizing their central nervous systems in controlling their bodies. They theorized that if the central nervous system was put out of commission, then it could have no effect whatsoever on the responses of the inner body.

Using this method, Dr. Miller successfully trained rats, and then many other types of animals, to consciously manipulate their involuntary functions. The paralyzed animals could not eat, drink, or breathe. They were given air by means of a specially devised artificial respiratory system. And they were also rewarded with an electrical stimulation of the brain that produced extreme pleasure. Dr. Miller was able to teach the rats to manipulate and control various bodily responses. This was a giant step toward the discovery of bio-feedback techniques.

..*Brain Waves:* In 1924, a German physicist named Hans Berger discovered that the brain gives off waves in the form of electricity. This led the way to biofeedback. Dr. Berger believed that the brain stored energy in the form of electricity. This was considered revolutionary at the time. In spite of this, Dr. Berger set out with great enthusiasm to prove his claims.

The first success came after several years of research. Dr. Berger had used those years to develop a crude electrical-wave recording device sensitive enough to detect the minute electrical signals produced by the brain. In a major experiment this device was attached to a young mental patient, and Dr. Berger was able to establish the existence of two different types of brain waves. He called them *alpha* and *beta*. The alpha waves were recorded whenever the subject seemed to be in a state of relaxation or passivity. The beta waves were found to be connected with states of concentrated activity. The beta wave is the wave of highest fre-

169

quency and appears when the mind is alert. It is rapid and somewhat erratic.

The modern day electroencephalograph, or EEG, is directly descended from Dr. Berger's early device. It is a machine that uses electrodes, which are attached to the scalp of the subject. These electrodes pick up the brain waves, which are then amplified and relayed to another machine that traces the electrical activity onto a long moving roll of graph paper.

After the development of the modern EEG, two additional brain waves were discovered. These are called *theta* and *delta* waves. Theta waves are commonly associated with the period immediately prior to the onset of sleep. However, they are also connected with creative states, hallucination, and in some subjects, anxiety. Delta evidences the lowest rate of wave frequency and is normally associated with sleep.

Bio-feedback and the Brain: In 1958 a researcher named Joseph Kamiya, working at the University of Chicago, first hypothesized that it might be possible to teach a human subject to be aware of his brain patterns.[1] Dr. Kamiya began an experiment in which he attached an EEG machine to the head of an isolated subject. When a bell rang, the subject was to say whether or not he felt himself to be in the alpha state. After his guess, he was immediately told the correct answer. This provided the subject with a means of monitoring his brain-wave state and associating his mental and physical condition with that knowledge. At the conclusion of the first day of the experiment it was found that the subject had guessed correctly nearly half the time. And as the experiment progressed further progress was made. By the fourth day the subject was totally aware of whether or not he was in the alpha state. This experiment was repeated numerous times on other subjects, and the results were the same. Not only were the subjects able to learn when they were in the alpha state, they were also able to learn how to enter that state at will.

Dr. Kamiya immediately went about improving his techniques. By connecting a special device that produced a single tone, he was able to shorten the time it took for his subjects to exercise control over their alpha states. When the mind entered the alpha state, this tone would sound. Therefore, it was only necessary for the subject to learn how to produce the sound in order to realize that he or she was in the alpha state.

Since these initial experiments it has been found that the other three brain waves can also be controlled through bio-feedback. Its uses have been extended, and its possibilities begin to seem endless—especially in situations where subjects have totally resisted other types of therapy, as is the case with hardened chronic alcoholics. Bio-feedback training allows us to consciously control our moods, emotions and reactions to various types of experience.

The advantages and values of bio-feedback cannot be overestimated. It is a method which can put us in touch with the inner workings of our bodies and minds. It requires far less time and discipline than any of the Eastern meditative techniques, which makes it ideally suited for the modern American who is unwilling to devote her or himself to those more demanding and time-consuming disciplines. It offers a definite contribution toward maintaining good health and well being.

Bio-feedback training as an adjunct to preventive medicine is not a far-fetched idea. It is not even very far away from being a reality. At present an enormous amount of research into the benefits of bio-feedback is being conducted despite the usual controversy surrounding the introduction of any new scientific discipline. The argument for bio-feedback training is that it can help a patient to eradicate a health problem by locating the organ or part of the body in which the health problem exists. Once this has been accomplished, it appears to be relatively easy to train the mind to combat the difficulty.

In Boston, Thomas Mulholland is investigating bio-feedback as a means of discovering and treating brain disease and malfunction. Joseph Kamiya believes that those suffering from mental disorders could use bio-feedback to learn to behave in a more healthy, normal fashion. Bio-feedback is also thought to be a viable alternative to the use of tranquilizers and other drugs. It is also hoped that bio-feedback might be valuable as an alternative to anesthesia.

The fact that bio-feedback does work has been made clear in a study on a subject of major concern: hypertension. Drug therapy has not yet proved completely successful in the treatment of hypertensive diseases. Although weight reduction and regular exercise have been useful in reducing dangerous levels of blood pressure when obesity is a major contributing factor, these methods are frequently not sufficient to correct the problem. It is in this area that bio-feedback, in conjunction with a revised life style, has proved effective.[2]

Patients are trained, using light-and-sound feedback, to "hear" their blood pressure. Herbert Benson, working at Harvard University, has been particularly successful in this area. Dr. Benson has reported success in five out of seven cases.

After learning to monitor the blood pressure, the next step is for hypertensive persons to be trained to control their blood pressure without feedback from machines. Surprisingly enough, progress has been slowed because of the resistance most Westerners brings to the concept of tuning their minds inward to hear a natural process of the body such as their blood pressure.[6]

MEDITATION

Meditation has been mentioned many times in the first part of this chapter. Eastern meditative techniques have been used as the basis for many of the theories concerning bio-feedback. Researchers working in several areas have been eager to discover whether the physical and mental control evidenced by the practitioners of meditation can be scientifically explained. In light of recent discoveries in the fields of brain function and subsequent research into the techniques of bio-feedback, it has become clear that the claims of many Eastern meditative practitioners are valid.

By utilizing bio-feedback machinery, scientists have been able to monitor the changes that occur during meditative practices. The practitioners of Eastern disciplines, however, deny that bio-feedback can be of value in achieving the inner awareness and peace that are the goals of their religious practices. But this controversy is not in the scope of this book. Let us, instead, examine some of these Eastern disciplines and see how they resemble the current bio-feedback system.

Yoga: Practitioners of yoga claim to be able to control their blood temperature, which enables them to endure extreme cold. They are able to fast for great lengths of time. And they can hold their breath for hours. In 1935 Theresa Bosse, a French cardiologist, working in India, determined to discover whether or not there was any valid scientific basis for these claims. The subjects she selected were yogis, practitioners of yoga, who claimed that they could stop their hearts. Using a small portable electrocardiograph, Dr. Bosse found that at least one of the subjects could indeed stop his heart. The technique he used is known as *Valasava*. In this, the breath is held and the muscles of the thorax are contracted while the meditator focuses his concentration downward. Unfortunately, later experimenters have been unable to duplicate Dr. Bosse's results. But they have been able to prove that yogis can greatly reduce their heartbeat and respiration levels through mental control.[5]

Zen Meditation: Practitioners of Zen meditation can

173

also slow their metabolisms. This has been proven many times. Dr. Y. Sugi and Dr. K. Akatsu conducted one study in which a number of meditating Zen monks were found to be able to reduce their need for oxygen by almost 20 per cent.

In another study, conducted at Tokyo University, forty-eight Zen masters and their disciples were observed during meditation. After approximately fifty seconds, the alpha state appeared in all. This occured whether the eyes were closed or not. This was immediately followed by an increase in amplitude of the alpha waves, which could conceivably be related to the deepening of the meditative state. At the same time, the alpha frequency decreased. In some subjects the frequency level became so slow that the meditators began to evidence theta waves. It was this theta state that the Zen master considered to be most indicative of deep meditation.

The final goal of Zen meditation is to reach a condition wherein the mind is totally free of all attachments and completely unconscious of self.

Transcendental Meditation: TM is an adaptation of yoga. It is quite similar to Zen meditation. Although the spiritual goals of these disciplines are not always similar, they still share some of the same types of vigorous mental exercises.

In both cases these meditative techniques take time, practice, and self-discipline.

TM has become extremely popular in the United States during the past few years. It involves no specific religious beliefs or life style. It is easily learned in far less time than most other forms of meditation. It might be described as a marriage between Eastern mysticism and Western popular deductive thought. TM emphasizes practical considerations. It is, therefore, particularly attractive to the Western mind.

Basically, the goal of TM is to bring the meditator into harmony with the universe. This is accomplished by focusing the concentration on some particular thing, in most cases, a nonsense-syllable sound which is called a *mantra.* The repetition of this mantra induces a receptive state that contributes to the achievement of a specific goal, such as relaxation of tension, or lowering blood pressure. A shallower state of breathing results which lowers the amount of carbon dioxide in the blood plasma and thus reduces the energy needs of the body. This process brings about the state of extreme calm and restful contemplation that was sought. When practicing TM, the mediator exhibits EEG patterns similar to those shown by yogis and Zen monks. These mental states are also desirable in the practice of bio-feedback.

The benefits of meditation cannot be denied. TM and bio-feedback or any of the religious meditative disciplines can definitely decrease tension, both physical and mental. They can produce tranquility, and they can increase energy and the ability to perform concentrated work. The possibilities presented by meditative techniques to the health fields, especially in such areas as the treatment of alcoholics, are quite profound.

Practitioners of TM generally report improved health, notably in those areas most affected by stress. In one study, 384 questionnaires were sent out to practitioners of TM. Three-hundred-thirty-three of the respondants spoke of an improved state of mental health. Twenty-nine said that they had suffered fewer headaches, seven said that their blood pressure had been reduced since they had taken up meditation.

In another study, researchers Wallace and Benson made a thorough investigation into the effects of meditation on drug abuse in order to discover whether or not the meditation had any effect on drug use. They divided their questionnaire into separate time frames. It was then mailed out to 1,950 meditators. It was found that in the six-month period prior to becoming involved in TM, 80 per cent of the subjects who answered the questionnaire had used marijuana, 48 per

cent had used LSD, 38 per cent had used amphetamines, 27 per cent had used barbiturates.

After six months of meditating, the results were quite
dramatic. Only 37 per cent were still using marijuana.
As time progressed, there was a steady decline in marijuana use until, after twenty-two months, only one
meditator was still using the drug heavily, 12 per cent
still used it occasionally. In the case of LSD, only 11
per cent of the meditators formerly involved with the
drug still reported its use. The reduction in use of other
types of drugs was equally dramatic.[3]

Summary: It would seem that reduction of anxiety
and tension, coupled with increased self-awareness
might be the answer to the question of alcohol and
other types of drug addition. All of these can be
brought about through meditative techniques including
TM, and also through bio-feedback. In addition, a
sense of self-mastery results from the necessary self-
discipline involved, which is of considerable psychological value.

Tension is relieved very easily through the use of
bio-feedback devices. If tension relief is the answer to
alcoholism, this method could be of incredible value.

Naturally, these ideas are quite controversial. They
have yet to be fully tested. However, it is well known
that psychosomatic disease can be just as dangerous as
physical disease. Therefore, it would seem that a
method of treating the emotional causes of illness could
be of great benefit. This is exactly what bio-feedback
and TM are designed to do. They teach the patient to
modify emotional reactions so that psychological stress
will not perpetuate destructive patterns of behavior. If
anxiety and stress can be obliterated it is hoped that
both mental and physical health can be maintained.

REFERENCES AND ADDITIONAL READING FOR CHAPTER NINE

1. Kamiya, J., *On Bio-feedback and Self-Control*, Aldine-Atherton, Inc., Chicago, Illinois, 1971.
2. Sargent, J., *et al.*, "The Use of Autogenic Feedback Training in a Pilot Study of Migraine and Tension Headaches," *Headache*, 12:120-124, 1972.
3. Wallace, R. K., "Physiological Effects of Transcendental Meditation," *Science*, 167:1751-1754, 1970.
4. Allison, J., "Respiratory Changes During the Practice of the Technique of Transcendental Meditation," *Lancet*, 7651, 1970.
5. Anand, B., *et al.*, "Some Aspects of EEG Studies on Yogis," *Electroencephelogram and Clinical Neurology*, 13, 1961.
6. Benson, H., "Yoga for Drug Abuse," *New England Journal of Medicine*, November, 1969.
7. Taft, C. T., *Altered States of Consciousness*, Wiley, New York, 1969.

FURTHER READING

1. *Alcohol and Health: New Knowledge*, Second special report to the U.S. Congress, Public Health Service, The Secretary of Health, Education and Welfare, June, 1974.
2. LaBianca, D. A., *Acetaldehyde Syndrome and Alcoholism*, The New School of Liberal Arts, Brooklyn College of the City University of New York, Brooklyn, New York, October, 1974.
3. Arky, R. A., "Influences of Alcohol on the Anabolic Phase of Carbohydrate Metabolism," *Biology of Alcoholism*, Vol. 1, Chap. 6.
4. Abramson, E. A., Arky, R. A., "Acute Antilipolytic Effects of Ethyl Alcohol and Acetate in Man," *Journal of Laboratory Clinical Medicine*, 72:105, 1968.
5. Ashmore, J., Weber, G., *Carbohydrate Metabolism and Its Disorders*, Vol. 1, pp. 336-375, Academic Press, London, 1968.
6. Fry, M. M., *et al.*, "Intensification of Hypertriglyceridemia by Either Alcohol or Carbohydrate," *American Journal of Clinical Nutrition*, Vol. 26, No. 8, August, 1973.
7. Rosenthal, W. S., *et al.*, "Riboflavin Deficiency in Complicated Chronic Alcoholism," *American Journal of Clinical Nutrition*, Vol. 26, No. 8, August, 1973.
8. Williams, R. J., *Alcoholism: The Nutritional Approach*, University of Texas Press, Austin, Texas, 1959.
9. Flink, E. B., "Mineral Metabolism in Alcoholism," *Biology of Alcoholism*, Vol. 1, 1970.
10. Sullivan, J. F., *et al.*, "Magnesium Metabolism in Alcoholism," *American Journal of Clinical Nutrition*, Vol. 13, November, 1963.
11. Myers, R. D., *et al.*, "The Determinents of Alcohol Preference in Animals," *Physiology and Behavior*, Vol. 2, 1972.

12. Burgess, L. B., *Alcohol and Your Health*, Charles Publications, Los Angeles, California, 1973.

13. Milt, H., "Nutritional Theory," *Basic Handbook on Alcoholism*, Scientific Aides Publications, New Jersey, 1974.

14. Rodgers, D. A., "Nutritional Effects on Alcohol Preference," *Biology of Alcoholism*, Vol. 2, Chapter 5.

15. Jones, B. M., Parsons, O. A., "Getting High, Coming Down," *Psychology Today*, January, 1975.

16. "Orientals and Alcohol," *Time Magazine*, New York, October 22, 1973.

17. Pawan, G. L. S., "Metabolism of Alcohol (Ethanol) in Man," *Procedures in Nutritional Sociology*, 31:83, 1972.

18. Westerfeld, W. W., Schulman, M. P., "Metabolism and Caloric Value of Alcohol," *Journal of the American Medical Association*, Vol. 170, No. 2, May 9, 1959.

19. Tremolieres, J., *et al.*, "Metabolic Effects of Ethanol," *Procedures in Nutritional Sociology*, 31:107, 1972.

20. Sardesai, V. M., Orten, J. M., "Effect of Prolonged Alcohol Consumption in Rats on Pancreatic Synthesis," *Nutrition*, 96:241-46, May 10, 1968.

21. Gabuzda, G. J., Shear, L., "Metabolism of Dietary Protein in Hepatic Cirrhosis," *American Journal of Clinical Nutrition*, Vol. 23, No. 4, April, 1970.

22. Orten, J. M., Sardesai, V. M., "Inter-relationships Between Protein and Alcohol Metabolism," *Biology of Alcoholism*, Vol. 1, Chapter 7.

23. Vitale, J. J., Coffey, J., "Alcohol and Vitamin Metabolism," *Biology of Alcoholism*, Vol. 1, 1970.

24. Morley, N. H., Clarke, D. W., "Influence of Ethanol and Talbutamide on Carbohydrate Metabolism in the Dog," *Quarterly Journal of Studies in Alcoholism*, Vol. 28. No. 4, 1967.

25. Badawy, A., Evans, M., "Alcohol and Tryptophan Metabolism," *Journal of Alcoholism*, Vol. 9, No. 3, Autumn, 1974.

26. O'Keane, M., *et al.*, "Ascorbic Acid Status of Alcoholics," *Journal of Alcoholism*, Vol. 7, No. 1, Spring, 1972.

27. Leevy, C. M., *et al.*, "B-complex Vitamins in Liver Disease of the Alcoholic," *American Journal of Clinical Nutrition*, Vol. 16, No. 4, April, 1965.

28. Lee, M., Lucia, S. T., "Effect of Ethanol on the Mobilization of Vitamin A in the Rat," *Quarterly Journal of Studies in Alcoholism*, Vol. 26, No. 1, March, 1965.

29. Senter, R. J., Sinclaire, J. D., "Thiamin-Induced Alcohol Consumption in Rats," *Quarterly Journal of Studies in Alcoholism*, Vol. 29, No. 2, June, 1968.

30. Blackstock, E. E., *et al.*, "The Role of Thiamin Deficiency in the Aetiology of the Hallucinatory States Complicating Alcoholism," *British Journal of Psychiatry*, 121:357-64, 1972.

31. Gordon, E. S., *Nutritional and Vitamin Therapy in General Practice*, Yearbook Publishers, Inc., Chicago, Illinois, 1947.

32. Leevy, C. M., Baker, H., "Vitamins and Alcoholism," *American Journal of Clinical Nutrition*, Vol. 21, No. 11, November, 1968.

33. Adamson, R., Black, R., "Volitional Drinking and Avoidance Learning in the White Rat," *Journal of Comprehensive Physiological Psychology*, 52:734, 1959.

34. Arvola, A., Forsander, O., "Comparison Between Water and Alcohol Consumption in Six Animal Species in Free-Choice Experiments," *Nature*, 191:819, 1961.

35. Brady, R. A., Westerfeld, W. W., "The Effect of B-Complex Vitamins on the Voluntary Consumption of Alcohol by Rats," *Quarterly Journal of Studies in Alcoholism*, 7:499, 1947.

36. Casey, A., "The Effect of Stress on the Consumption of Alcohol and Reserpine," *Quarterly Journal of Studies in Alcoholism*, 21:208, 1960.

37. Baum, R., Iber, F. L., "Alcohol, the Pancreas, Pancreatic Inflammation, and Pancreatic Insufficiency," *American Journal of Clinical Nutrition*, Vol. 26, No. 3, March, 1973.

38. Murdock, H. R., "Thyroidal Effect of Alcohol," *Quarterly Journal of Studies in Alcoholism*, Vol. 28, No. 3, September, 1967.

181

39. Marks, V., Chakraborty, J., "The Clinical Endocrinology of Alcoholism," *Journal of Alcoholism*, Vol. 8, No. 3, Autumn, 1973.

40. Axelrod, D. R., "Metabolic and Endocrine Aberrations in Alcoholism," *Biological Basis of Alcoholism*.

41. Gardiner, R. J., Stewart, H. B., "Blood Alcohol and Glucose Changes after Ingestion of Ale, Wine and Spirit," *Quarterly Journal of Studies in Alcoholism*, Vol. 29, No. 2, June, 1969.

42. Ashworth, C. T., *et al.*, "Hepatic Lipids," *Archives of Pathology*, 72:625, 1961.

43. Bizzi, A., *et al.*, "Trygliceride Accumulation in Liver," *Nature*, 209:1025, 1966.

44. Chappell, J. B., "Systems Used for the Transport of Substrates into Mitochondria," *British Medical Bulletin*, 24:150, 1969.

45. Crouse, J. R., Gerson, C. D., DeCarli, L. M., Lieber, C. S., "Role of Acetate in the Reduction of Plasma-Free Fatty Acids Produced by Alcohol in Man," *Journal of Lipid Research*, 9:509, 1968.

46. Rutter, L. F., "A Study of Lactate and Pyruvate Levels in Blood and Urine Samples from Abstinant Alcoholics and Their Biochemical Significance," *Journal of Alcoholism*, Vol. 6, No. 2, Summer, 1971.

47. Lindenbaum, J., "Hematologic Effects of Alcohol," *Biology of Alcoholism*, Vol. 3, Clinical Pathology, 1974.

48. Crux-Coke, R., "Genetic Aspects of Alcoholism," *Biological Basis of Alcoholism*.

49. French, S. W., "Acute and Chronic Toxicity of Alcohol," *Biology of Alcoholism*, Vol. 1, Chap. 14.

50. Maisel, A. Q., "Alcohol and Your Brain: Some News for Social Drinkers," *Reader's Digest*, June, 1970.

51. Sullivan, J. F., *et al.*, "Myocardiopathy of Beer Drinkers: Subsequent Course," *Annals of Internal Medicine*, September 23, 1968.

52. Dreyfys, P. M., "Diseases of the Nervous System in Chronic Alcoholism," *Biology of Alcoholism*, Vol. 3, Clinical Pathology, 1974.

53. Kissin, B., Kaley, M. M., *Alcohol and Cancer*, SUNY Downstate Medical Center, Brooklyn.

54. Greer, F. G., "Hypoglycemia of Hypo-Adrenocorticism and Alcoholism," *Journal of Alcoholism*, Vol. 7, No. 4, Winter, 1972.

55. "Alcoholic Myopathy," *The New England Journal of Medicine*, June 9, 1966.

56. Mayer, R. F., Garcia-Mullin, R., "Peripheral Nerve and Muscle Disorders Associated with Alcoholism," Vol. 2, Chap. 2.

57. Song, S. K., Rubin, E., "Ethanol-Produced Muscle Damage in Human Volunteers," *Science*, Vol. 175, pp. 327-8, January 21, 1972.

INDEX

185